Lady

Roosh Valizadeh

Table of Contents

To my sister

Prologue

"You hate women!" This accusation has been thrown at me hundreds of times. Because I've been critical of women in my writing, and I've wanted to improve them in some way, I must therefore "hate" them. Personally, I know I don't hate women. I've spent a big chunk of my life learning how to better connect with them, and I've given advice to tens of thousands of men with the aim of making women feel attracted to them. It's still impossible to refute the accusation that "I hate women," because you cannot prove to someone that hatred disguised as critique does not lie buried within your soul. If one follows this line of reasoning, anyone who has criticized anything at some point must have done so out of hatred, meaning that I also "hate" men, every country I've traveled to, exercise, pugs, and even myself.

My "hatred" of men must be especially strong because most of my work has had the aim of unlocking inner barriers that prevent them from becoming stronger, more interesting men that women find attractive. This work stems from my own transformation from a 22-year-old college graduate who knew nothing about women to a 39-year-old man who has had just about every imaginable experience with them. My advice to both men and women is ultimately borne from idealism: if men can embrace their natural masculinity, and women can embrace their natural femininity, things would be better for everyone, and we could avoid the negative aspects of modern culture, such as meaningless hookups and sterile relationships. Perhaps my ideal of how the sexes should relate can never be achieved, but I think we can get pretty close.

At this point, I'm supposed to convince you that I'm an "expert," and that you will be doomed to a life of unhappiness and loneliness if you don't follow my advice, but I am not an expert. I have no fancy psychology degrees. I'm merely a man who has lived richly without delusions and come to see the truth of male-female bonding. My hope is that you're about to read what you have subconsciously identified as the truth but have not been able to articulate. I doubt I'll reveal anything that isn't already contained within your being. The task of a teacher is not to implant new ideas into a student's mind but to set out reality so plainly and clearly that the student naturally discovers the truth on his or her own.

Lady marks the first time I'm writing directly to women instead of men. This is a challenge for me because each sex prefers a unique style of communication. Men prefer direct communication that is dense in facts and logic. We place a high value on the quality of information as opposed to the quantity. Women are different. They engage more in indirect communication that is full of hints, suggestions, and metaphors that contribute to an overall mood or feeling. A conversation with a woman is like a ballet that can have multiple interpretations, a fact that has frustrated men for millennia. Women prefer to receive communication indirectly, dropped delicately from the noise, while avoiding negative emotions that make them feel like they are being threatened or judged. Men prefer to get to the point quickly and directly, at the risk of hurting the feelings of others or even their own.

In preparation for writing this book, I skimmed other books that were written for women. The writing was quite soft and flowery, with an annoying over-abundance of metaphors. Within each page I found myself saying "Get to the point!" but I understand that the point isn't the point—

it's more to do with keeping the female reader in a favorable emotional state. As a veteran writer, I think I could mimic this style, but I fear you will miss my conclusions or misinterpret them. Therefore, you may encounter passages that challenge your mood, your worldview, and how you see yourself as a woman. Your first instinct will be denial, that what I'm writing is simply not true, and then you will feel angry. You may even yell "He hates women!" as a self-protection mechanism to avoid accepting that you may possess flaws or blind-spots that are hurting you. This is okay. Accept the information you want and discard the rest that feels painful, although I'm confident that, in time, you will be able to accept the truths I share.

In life, there is a time for hearing "sweet little lies," as the Fleetwood Mac song tells us, and there is a time for knowing the truth so that you can improve your life. I would rather tell you the hard truth and have you resent me for it than tell you sweet lies that merely entertain you or don't challenge you enough to solve your problems. That said, if at some point you throw this book across the room and send an email to me saying that you wish I would die, I won't take it personally. I'm writing this with a softer hand than I use in my books for men, but it will ultimately be up to you to judge whether it was soft enough.

I'll end this prologue by sharing why I decided to write a book for women, years after becoming infamous as the "world's biggest misogynist," a term the Washington Post has used to describe me. First, I kept getting emails from women thanking me for my writing. Most of them were in their late twenties or early thirties, and had reached a stage where they had uncovered the lie that they would be fulfilled by dedicating most of their lives to careers for the purpose of accumulating material possessions instead of focusing on family. These emails, which have increased in frequency over the years, tell me that I would help women better if I addressed them directly.

The second reason I've written this book is that the men I've aided with self-improvement are faced with a culture where women haven't improved themselves, and who have in fact declined. I'm telling men to increase their value to be the best men they can, but after they complete this tough personal journey, they venture out and discover that women are worse than they were a few years ago. Sadly, there are no positive role models for women in entertainment, mass media, government, and the universities. These institutions teach women how to be impulsive, masculine, vulgar, and promiscuous while pushing them to become enslaved in the rat race to prove that they are "as good as men" or that they don't "need" a man. This makes it virtually impossible for a woman to create a loving family.

I admit there is something amusing about the "world's biggest misogynist" attempting to help women be happier, but it makes sense from my perspective. If the establishment is harming women by encouraging them to lead a degenerate lifestyle that is a one-way ticket to getting hooked on anti-depressant pills, the *opposite* of what it says may very well be the answer. If the establishment is promoting a feminist author for her book on "female empowerment," and she appears on all the mainstream talk shows, you should do the exact opposite of what she says. On the other hand, if the establishment is rabidly denouncing a writer as being hateful to women, without providing a logical reason why, that man may be speaking the truth.

Ultimately, my mission with this book is to help you have a better life as a woman, at the risk of hurting your feelings or forcing you to accept that you've made mistakes in the past. As a man who has made countless mistakes, particularly in my pursuit of casual sex for more than a decade, I know that it's what we learn from our mistakes that will enable us to live better lives. It's okay to accept that we've messed up in the past, but now are getting on the right path, wiser than before. So let's get started.

LADY

Book I: You

Happiness

I chafe when people ask me, "Are you happy?" It's complicated, I want to reply, because we should question if happiness is a goal worth pursuing when it's so easy to adapt to any emotional state we face, whether negative or positive. The problem with seeking happiness is that you have to keep adding "happy things" to your life until inevitably you cannot obtain anything new that will exceed the highs of before.

Imagine that right now I give you a new mansion with no strings attached. How will you feel when you first walk into the mansion? Unless you already live in a mansion, you will feel like you just won the lottery, and thank me profusely for changing your life as you dream of all the lovely furniture and decorations you plan to fill the house with.

Fast forward five years. You've spent almost 2,000 nights in the mansion and have become accustomed to it. What happens when you walk into the mansion now? Because you've adapted to it, nothing happens. You don't feel an emotional rush or a surge of happiness. You long ago took the house for granted, just like you take for granted the air you're breathing in right now. If the goal of your life really is happiness, you will continually have to swap your mansion for an even bigger mansion to experience new bursts of happiness.

When I was in my early twenties, I would get a high every time I slept with a new woman. I concluded that if I slept with *a lot* of women, I'd be *really* happy, so I structured my life to have a constant supply of new women. As you might expect, I adapted to casual sex. Then the sex had to be novel in some way—the girl had to be from a different country, or I had to speak to her in a foreign language, or I had to sleep with her within a certain time frame as if I were competing in an Olympic event. By the time I came up with the idea to sleep with two new girls in one night, I knew that I had hit a wall.

If your goal is perpetual happiness, you will be forced to seek out an escalating ladder of situations or objects that merely give you *bursts* of happiness, and when those bursts fade because of your ability to adapt, you will seek out a new set of situations or objects to experience a renewed burst. This cycle will repeat itself until your ability to experience new bursts of happiness diminishes and you hit a wall, as I did. Then you will begin the pity party of "I have bad luck" and "Life is not fair," even though, objectively, you have clothes, food, shelter, and enough disposable income to enjoy the type of leisure that most people in the world do not.

Most women feel unhappy because it's becoming difficult or impossible for them to have new experiences that produce more novelty, excitement, luxury, or fun than their past experiences. This happens soon after a woman has passed the peak of her beauty or fertility. Once a woman's beauty starts to decline, she will find it harder to be happier than when she was young and received more positive attention from men. For men, peak happiness usually coincides with the height of their wealth, health, or fame.

One clue that you're pursuing distorted happiness is having goals that, once you attain them, result in you setting a new goal that simply involves chasing more of what you have just gained. For example, if your goal is to earn a salary of $100,000 a year, what will happen if you hit that goal? If you're like most people, you will then aim for a higher salary, such as $200,000. If your goal is to get 100 likes on a selfie, what will you do once you hit this number? Aim for 200 likes or more. Setting numerical goals puts you on a never-ending treadmill, because numbers can go to infinity, and you will always know many people who have reached bigger numbers. If you allow your mind to convince you that your happiness depends on hitting a certain numerical goal, you will eventually become a slave to numbers, and you won't be any happier in the end.

Even non-numerical goals can be dangerous. Today, your goal may be to live in a certain style of apartment in the center of the city, but once you've lived there for a while, you will ache to live in a bigger, more luxurious apartment in an even better area. Today, you may want a certain outfit that you saw a celebrity wearing, but after buying it, you come down from your high and want to buy another outfit. Once you've achieved a level of material security, such as having food and shelter, objects that exist outside of you cannot consistently provide long-term fulfillment or happiness. Instead, they keep you running on the treadmill. This also includes sex and altered mental states produced by alcohol or drugs, both legal and illegal.

It may be hard to accept that the material world cannot make you happy, because society has trained you since you were a child to seek happiness through material fulfillment, especially through money, physical pleasure, and fame, but the message of "If I can gain this thing, I will be happy" is an illusion. The reality is this: "If I can gain this thing, I will be happy for a brief moment, and then I will want to gain another thing." It's only once you get off the treadmill of materialism and realize that nothing outside of you can provide lasting happiness, all because of your human ability to adapt, that you can begin to be content with life.

How has happiness become the goal of our culture if pursuing it does not lead to sustained happiness? The answer is money. If I can convince you that you're not happy, but that you will be happy if you buy my shiny new product or use my social app, isn't it in my best interests to teach you that happiness can be gained only through materialism? There are trillions of dollars at stake in the consumer economy, mostly based on selling you happiness, and when you consider that most of the world's wealth is controlled by a handful of elite individuals and corporations, it's not hard to see why it's so advantageous to convince everyone that happiness can be bought.

Believing in the idea of "If I can gain this thing, I will be happy" keeps you running on a treadmill for your entire life, working just hard enough to buy a new condo, car, or electronic toy. If I were a member of the elite club and had a big stake in corporations that produced gadgets, makeup, and clothing, why would I teach you that happiness is actually more of a spiritual essence or feeling when doing so would cost me millions or billions of dollars in lost profit? Instead, I would pay my allies in the media, government, and universities to attack and isolate any man or group that says materialism is a foolish pursuit, or that there is something wrong with the current way of doing things. I wouldn't want anyone to rock the boat if I was getting rich off the deception.

An important question worth asking yourself: why should you be happy? Where is it written or mandated that human beings should exist in a state of emotional happiness? If you believe in God, you know that we lost our chance to be happy when Eve ate from the Tree of the Knowledge of Good and Evil, and if you don't believe in God and accept that evolution explains how humans came about, imagine how easy it would have been to kill constantly happy humans who were more likely to miss the serious threats to their existence in a primal environment of scarce food, poisonous snakes, and falling trees. A happy human in a dangerous environment would soon be a dead human, unlike one who is more careful and alert.

Whether we were created or evolved, there is no indication that the goal of our existence is happiness. We must conclude that happiness is a modern construct designed to sell you products and keep you running on the treadmill. It's quite an ingenious scam. As a member of the elite, I can pay people in Hollywood, the advertising industry, and the media to push the idea that happiness is a worthy goal that can be attained through products or entertainment. Then I have my partners in big companies employ women under the guise of "equality" while dangling the stick of "empowerment" so women will work hard for a meager wage, all because they believe they need products and other forms of stimulation to be happy. When the treadmill fails them, and it will, I then get my friends in pharmaceutical companies to sell these unhappy women anti-depressants that turn them into automatons that have just enough strength to continue working at their unfulfilling jobs. At the same time, journalists can write articles about how "strong" women are having casual sex with men they barely know under the influence of alcohol, and gush about the fun "egg-freezing" parties they throw in their late thirties.

All the while, strong families are not being created, which means I don't have to worry about tribes of strong men with loyal sons overthrowing the status quo. Both men and women have become weak, cosmopolitan, and atomized. They chase consumer products while enslaved to soul-destroying jobs, various substances, and cheap sex.

Human Nature

If we're not meant to be happy, what is the purpose of our lives? The most reasonable answer is to exist according to our nature. If you're a man, this means doing masculine things, and if you're a woman, this means doing feminine things. To complete the circle of masculine-feminine polarity, your instinct is to seek the complement to your femininity and pair-bond or reproduce with the masculine. Of course there's more to life than merely surviving and reproducing. We like to laugh, listen to music, appreciate good food, marvel at beauty, play games, and engage in other activities that make us feel part of our tribe or culture, but it's hard to enjoy these activities to the fullest if our primary purpose is not being satisfied.

The second aspect of our purpose is to overcome difficulties in harsh environments. Either God created us to live in a world that was harder to survive than it is today or, because we evolved in a life-threatening environment, our DNA equips us to deal with dangerous situations. Our problem is that modern society has made it too easy to merely survive, to the point where there is practically no chance that we will starve to death or be killed by the elements.

Our original nature prepared us to be constantly anxious about the threats in our environment, but now that most of those threats are gone, we're anxious about things that don't threaten our survival. We get stressed out by a mild health symptom, an unexpected home repair, how we think people will see us at a party, or why a particular man or woman doesn't like us. If you think about the things that have caused you stress in the past month, it's likely that not one of them posed an immediate or acute threat to your survival. Unless you were in a horrific car accident or violently attacked, all your stress and anxiety arose from things that were not genuine threats.

If you're not in real danger, why do trivial matters make you feel anxious? Because you were built as an anxiety-generating machine that can survive in practically any harsh environment. For example, has it happened that you left home but couldn't remember whether or not you locked your door? You agonized over going back and checking, and if you weren't too far from home, you reluctantly returned and found that the door was indeed locked. From a natural standpoint, this anxiety is beneficial, because it can protect us from catastrophic events, but played out day after day in our safe and modern world, it can be crippling.

Every month, your mind will automatically produce a certain amount of anxiety, no matter your situation. Some people, due to their individual nature, produce more anxiety, whereas others produce less, but even if all your survival needs are met and there is nothing actually wrong with your life, you will still be anxious. Unless you drug your brain, which I don't recommend because of the side-effects, there is no way to stop being anxious. Instead, you must understand it. You can say, "Ah-ha! You're producing anxiety because it is encoded into my being, but there is no threat right now, so I will not strengthen you by looking for assurances." When you seek out information or knowledge to relieve your anxiety, you actually feed it. Anxiety survives on attention—the more you give it, the stronger it becomes. Instead, the best response is to allow the anxiety to happen, not feed it by seeking out assurances, and watch it starve of its own accord after a few days or even hours.

I'm sure you can see how useful anxiety is for focusing your attention on something that could harm you. In the past, a woman was in real danger of starving to death or being attacked by male warriors from other tribes. Not only did women live with this constant fear, but if a neighboring tribe did attack, her husband would be murdered, she would be raped, and she would be forced to start a new family with her rapist.

Modern feminists would have you believe that this sort of "rape culture" still exists, where Western women are being raped at a higher rate than women living in poor African slums, but the fact is that you can walk alone at night with only a minuscule chance of being attacked by a stranger, something that was virtually impossible a few generations ago.

If rates of rape, violence, and starvation are lower than they were in the past, what threats do you face today? The biggest is dropping your smartphone in the toilet bowl. Since this is the main device you use to communicate with friends and document your life, you will be extremely upset during the time it takes to replace your phone. The second biggest threat is being rejected by an attractive man, particularly one who disappeared after having sex with you. These things can be acutely stressful, but in the grand scheme of things they are minor and do not threaten your survival.

If you break your phone, you can take actionable steps of going to the store and getting a new one, but there is often nothing you can do about romantic problems, especially if the man has firmly decided that he does not want to be with you. Attempts to "think" your way out of the problem just makes you more stressed. In fact, you can't think your way out of any problem unless it results in taking action that puts you one step closer to a resolution.

If the things that are happening to you today don't threaten your survival, it's best to brush them off as life's normal inconveniences or disappointments instead of internalizing them as a sign that your life is bad. It's a big step from "It sucks that my phone broke" or "It sucks that Chad doesn't like me" to "My phone broke, so my life is horrible" or "Chad doesn't like me, so I will die alone." The former attitude accepts the reality that bad things happen in life, whereas the latter allows fleeting, short-term events to define your entire existence.

Ironically, if you do face a genuine threat to your survival, you'll be surprisingly calm when it happens. The anxiety acts as fuel to focus your attention on concrete action that eliminates the threat, which is exactly what nature intended, but if your survival is not actually threatened, and there is no concrete action step you can take, the anxiety doesn't get burned up as fuel, and its noxious fumes start to make you sick. The result is that you worry endlessly, convince yourself that you're not a happy person, and look for a harmful material "solution" to suppress the anxiety.

Problems that can't be responded to with concrete action push you towards materialism to feel better in the moment, at the cost of your health or long-term well-being. Because you live in modern society, you are most likely stuck in a vicious cycle of feeling anxious or unhappy and relieving this feeling temporarily through food, shopping, sexual attention, or drugs. Many of the harmful behaviors women engage in, such as emotional eating, binge drinking on the weekends, or hooking up with men who don't care about them, are futile attempts at alleviating a vague, nagging anxiety that does not put them in danger like being kidnapped and raped by warriors from other tribes.

The good news is that we will never be able to simulate ancient conditions where our survival was in near-constant threat. Thanks to modern technology, advanced food-production methods, and armed protection from the government, it is unlikely that we will die prematurely unless we're involved in a fatal car accident or contract a serious disease, outcomes that are far more abstract than starvation, rape, or war. To prevent starvation, you can harvest crops and store them properly, which will assure your survival, but to prevent a car accident, all you can do is wear a seat belt and hope that a driver doesn't randomly plow into you.

Today, we are unable to take concrete steps to limit our anxiety as we could in the past. This forces us to rely on materialism as a short-term fix, but this only makes things worse in the long run. The best answer is to understand how anxiety works and try to live according to our nature, whether masculine or feminine. By taking the huge step of understanding, we can begin to avoid the cycle of seeking out false solutions.

Our basic nature is to survive *and* pair-bond with our sexual opposite. At the very least, you are accomplishing the first one, assuming you don't get so triggered by my writing that you have a fatal heart attack. Before we can address pair-bonding, it's important to understand our sex-linked nature.

If humans were not made of two biological sexes, we'd be like bacteria and reproduce asexually through simple division. Instead, we have male and female, and barring an expensive fertility procedure in a laboratory, the male and female need to connect sexually and emotionally to produce children. To accomplish this end, nature gave men and women their own set of specific tools. Although there is some overlap in tool function, the differences are far more pronounced, ranging from physical abilities to ways of thinking. You may think it's unfair that there are things men can do that you can't, but when the masculine and the feminine are combined, there is nothing humans can't achieve. This combination has resulted in our species becoming the most dominant life form on Earth, of seven billion somewhat intelligent organisms who can explore space, control aspects of the environment, and write books like this.

But there's a catch: we have a bad side to our nature. For men, it is the unquenchable desire to have sex with multiple women. For women, it is the unquenchable desire to have sex with high-status men, where status can mean wealth, strength, fame, confidence, or attractiveness. The bad side of my nature wants me to sleep with as many beautiful women as I'm physically able to, and I did this for many years, but remember that we're also equipped with an adaptation program. I got used to sleeping with new women and became tired of it, but the bad side of my nature *still* insisted on more variety. This created a conflict where I couldn't bear to put in the work required for each additional lay, but I still wanted the decreasing reward. Imagine me as a fat man whose monstrous obesity left him so weak that he couldn't even stand up and walk to the refrigerator to get more food.

As a woman, the second you secure the commitment of a man you value, your nature will cause you to window shop for more men and test the field to see if another man who has higher status than your boyfriend will also commit to you. Since there will always be a higher-status man who is willing to at least have sex with you, though not necessarily commit to you, a woman who pursues the bad side of her nature will end up sabotaging *all* of her relationships. When a woman is in her early twenties and in the prime of her beauty, she may not have any trouble getting into a new relationship to replace a broken one, but once she enters her thirties, and the main bait she uses to hook the masculine—her beauty—is not as strong, she will find herself in a difficult situation.

I used to think that a new notch on my bedpost would make me happy, and many women think that getting a commitment from a high-status man will make them happy, but the second we achieve that new notch or commitment, the bad side of our nature tells us that we have to keep going to get yet another girl or another man of even higher status. The cycle doesn't end unless you consciously block it out by understanding that the negative side of your nature will put you on the road to suffering and loneliness.

What makes things even worse is that society teaches women to raise their own status by focusing on career as if they were men. I have lost count of how many times an American woman has tried to impress me with her job title as if this type of status is attractive to a masculine man. It isn't, because the masculine man craves making love to beauty, something he doesn't have, not to a career, which he likely already has. A man is more likely to desire a beautiful woman who is working at McDonald's than an ugly woman who is a high-powered attorney.

Some women have also adopted the masculine behavior of seeking notches, particularly men from foreign countries, thinking that that novelty will provide fulfillment, but it only damages their ability to have a monogamous relationship. If you consider that a woman is not even guaranteed to experience an orgasm from a casual sex act like a man is, it's hard to see how she benefits from a drunken hookup with someone who doesn't care about her.

When I would bring a new girl to my home from a nightclub, I would wonder why she was so willing to donate her body for far less gain than I was about to receive. The only explanation is that she was trying to relieve her anxiety, boredom, or unhappiness with a burst of sexual validation that faded in a day and left her less capable of bonding with a good man in the future.

When the culture teaches you that men and women are "equal," what it's really saying is that your nature is not linked to your biological sex. This softens you up so that you don't protest when you're forced to learn masculine traits, such as building your status through a career instead of enhancing your femininity and beauty. On the other end of the spectrum, men are embracing the feminine and becoming so obsessed with grooming and appearance that many women confuse them for being gay. In essence, we're teaching cats to bark like dogs and dogs to meow like cats. It's no surprise that neither sex is content.

You have three choices. The first is to buy into "equality" and deny your basic sex-linked nature, causing you to adopt the masculine and try to build up your status through a career and materialism. This will produce the most misery.

The second is to accept your nature but to feed those parts of it that demand you constantly seek higher-status men in a process that will result in being alone when you are older or ending up with a man who is nowhere close to your first choice. This will also make you miserable, but not as miserable as with the first choice.

The third choice is to *accept and understand* your nature, not let it sabotage you, and disconnect yourself from the materialistic roller-coaster ride of anxiety and fleeting happiness. This choice will produce the least misery, although life may still be difficult, because as I discussed earlier, nowhere is it decreed that experiencing pain and frustration aren't aspects of human life. The key word in this choice is "understand." You cannot totally defeat your feminine nature, just like how I cannot stop having sexual thoughts when I see a beautiful girl.

Not long ago, I was in a monogamous relationship. During this time, I had lustful thoughts about girls who were more beautiful than my already beautiful girlfriend, but these thoughts didn't mean there was a problem with my relationship. It was simply the bad side of my nature acting out. Fighting the lust by making myself feel guilty or ashamed wouldn't work, because I would just feed it further, keeping the idea of having sex with other women alive in my mind. I chose neither to fight it nor to act on it, and would wait hours or days for a lustful flare-up to subside. This is how I was able to remain faithful during the relationship.

In your case, once you get into a relationship, you may immediately start to doubt if your boyfriend is the best man you can get. You'll take action by window shopping for other men and flirting with them, which will inevitably lead to emotional or physical cheating. If acted on, the male instinct to lust after women is as damaging as your instinct to seek out higher-status men.

I could spend my entire life searching the world for more beautiful women to bed and never feel like I had finished. You can spend your entire life upgrading your man by finding another, yet there will still be millions of men who could be even better. It never ends! And by continuing to listen to the bad side of our nature, we will utterly fail to experience the immaterial bond of love between woman and man and also between woman and child through the creation of a family, which is the best way for humans to remove themselves from the shallow pursuit of sex, novelty, and status.

I have realized the importance of creating a family late in life. My chances of establishing one diminish with each passing year, so the best I can do is to warn others about the future they face if they don't look at their significant other and say, perhaps reluctantly, "This person is good enough," and step off the treadmill entirely, because if you let the bad side of your nature take hold, you're guaranteed to have a lonely outcome.

Think about the path of your life in the past few years. Do you feel like you're letting the bad side of your nature control your behavior, or have you been able to minimize its worst effects? If you've been able to minimize them, it's probably because someone has taken the time to teach you uncomfortable truths. It's encouraging to know that our deepest flaws can be minimized simply by understanding them. Not only does understanding remove feelings of guilt or shame, it also gives us the choice to ignore an instinct that, in the modern age, will lead to harm. Sometimes you'll lose out to the bad side of your nature and make the wrong choice, but in time you'll be able to treat a negative instinct like a stubborn fly that you can't quite manage to kill. Simply let the fly have its way until it dies of natural causes in a day or two.

Once you decide to ignore the bad side of your nature, you can pursue a goal that will maximize the joy you experience in life. This goal is to have a *practical* love with a man who believes you are the most beautiful woman he can reasonably get, minimizing the risk that he will stray from you, in a relationship that allows you to give birth to children whom you will deeply love.

Love *must* be part of our solution because it is immaterial unlike money, physical attractiveness, and even sex. One sign you know something is immaterial is if it still brings you joy after it has been taken away from you. If—God forbid—your husband or children die while you're alive, their memory will make you sad, but you will also feel immense happiness from having loved them and been part of their lives, even though their physical existence has ended. Outside of your husband and children, the only other way to experience immaterial love is having a deep relationship with God.

In other words, we should have listened to our grandparents. They were wiser than us because they nourished a practical love that resulted in creating a family, which kept them away from shallow temptations. *What would my grandmothers do?* If you stop reading this book right now and walk away with just this question, you will be better off. Since today's culture contains far more degeneracy than your grandmothers', you'll have to be that much stronger to overcome it and bond with one good man whose children you want to bear.

It's finally time for some positive news: we also have a good side to our sex-linked nature. For a man, it's wanting to provide food and shelter for his family and defend them with his life. Almost all men would sacrifice their lives for their families, especially their wives, without hesitation. For a woman, the good side of her nature is primarily to raise and nurture children and secondarily to please the man she loves. It is as instinctual for a man to trade his life for his family as it is for a woman to trade her life for her children.

To understand why you would never sacrifice your life for your husband's, we have to take a look at ancient history. When a village was invaded by a barbarian tribe, the men were killed first because they posed the greatest threat to the invaders. The women, however, were useful as kidnapped brides or slaves. To not be sold off as a slave, a woman "only" had to love the man who killed her husband and hope that he would step in and provide for her. Many women couldn't live with this arrangement and killed themselves or became slaves, but the ones who were able to love their barbarian husband went on to have more female descendants who also had the ability to love a barbarian rapist.

If you have rape fantasies, it's likely because you have a female ancestor who was raped and created a family with her rapist. It's why books such as *50 Shades of Grey* are international bestsellers. I don't condone rape or violence, but the reality is that a woman has the capacity to be with the man who forcefully took her after killing her husband.

Men, on the other hand, are ready to make the ultimate sacrifice for their families. With my most recent girlfriend, I was ready—at least subconsciously—to trade my life for hers. If we were robbed on the street by a knife-wielding maniac, I would tell her to run away while I distract the attacker, eliminating any danger for her while drastically increasing the chance that I would die. The alternative would be to use my girlfriend as a human shield by throwing her at the attacker, something that I've never heard of a man doing. The instinct for men to protect women is so strong that they try to save the lives of women who are complete strangers, and some men have even died doing so.

The good and bad sides of your nature are like having an angel on one shoulder and a devil on the other. Each is competing to control you. When you feel the instinct to cook an elaborate meal for your man or to otherwise please him, your angel is in control. When you upload a sexy selfie on social networking to get attention from men you hardly know, your devil is in control. When you evaluate a man for his stability and family values, your angel is in control. When you evaluate a man based on his body or fame, it's your devil.

Unfortunately, modern society is structured so you exclusively feed your devil, leaving your angel malnourished and in desperate need of essential vitamins and minerals. The only solution is to weaken your devil by restricting the behaviors that have given him power, but even if you do this, your devil will occasionally have surges of energy that test you when you least expect it, but just knowing that he's there, waiting to sabotage your life, is an important step to begin preventing his destructive influence.

I also have an angel and devil on my shoulders. The angel is telling me to *not* sleep around, create a family with a woman of good moral character, and be faithful. The devil is telling me to have sex with anything that gives me an erection, to travel the world in search of exotic and fun adventures, and to tell girls whatever they want to hear in order to sleep with them.

For fifteen years, my life was driven almost entirely by my devil, to the point where he became so morbidly obese and lethargic that my angel found a way to reassert himself and regain the upper hand. In my last relationship, my devil was still there, but the worst he could do was plant thoughts in my head that I didn't feel compelled to act on. The best outcome we can hope for is not to act on thoughts and suggestions from our devil while obeying those from our angel.

In your case, the best way to nurture the positive side of your nature is to get married, have children, and maintain a loving home in a way that makes both your husband and children feel blessed to have you in their lives. This certainly passes the "What would your grandmothers do?" test. Your angel will help you along this path as long as you ignore the devil feeding you thoughts of seeking high-status men, succumbing to fleeting pleasure with drugs and hookups, and attempting to relieve your anxiety through shopping or excessive eating. The inner fulfillment you crave can come only from the love created by having a family or a relationship with God. Otherwise, if you only listen to the bad side of your nature, you're doomed.

Why Feminism?

It turns out that feminism, and the idea of equality in general, are entirely dedicated to feeding your devil and *decreasing* the chance that you will get married, or if you happen to marry, stay happily married. If feminism feeds the negative side of female nature, why do all the major institutions support it? Why is it the default mentality among modern women? As I said earlier, the direct answer is money.

Feminism has two aims. First, it's to double the supply of labor in the workforce in order to reduce the price of wages. Second, it's to weaken the family unit so that women depend on corporations and government, which the elite control, instead of strong men.

You are being thrown under the bus so that men at the very top can make an extra billion in profits every year, and more money means more power. You're being manipulated by a group of ultra-rich oligarchs and their useful idiots in universities, government, and the media to have contempt for men and seek to become "independent" from them. They train you to put career, status, hedonism, and fame before love, family, and God, brainwashing you to think that normal men are trying to enslave you with child-raising and household chores. This causes you to voluntarily enslave yourself to corporate bosses and mass-produced consumer products.

Only a few decades ago, a husband could provide for his wife and children. Now, in most cases, both the husband and the wife have to work. Taking inflation into account, real household incomes have decreased since women entered the workforce. This is by design. Lower labor costs mean that companies can make larger profits, particularly for their executives and institutional shareholders. Once women had been programmed to pursue a career instead of a family, thereby flooding the workforce, the next step in the elite's plan was to open the borders so that millions of economic migrants could lower wages even more. Soon, you'll have to compete with the entire third world to earn a basic living.

In the past, a woman had the *option* of working or becoming a housewife, but now working has become an obligation that is disguised as "independence" and "empowerment," whereas it's anything but. There is nothing independent about being forced to do something that virtually every other woman is also doing. The modern woman has traded listening to a man at home, who loves her and would sacrifice his life for her, for following orders dictated by a man in an office, who can fire her for any reason and who has zero stake in her long-term well-being. That doesn't sound like an empowering trade-off to me.

In a traditional marriage, your husband was the main source of guidance and instruction. He would instinctively know what was best for the home, serving as your leader to get the family through hard times. Today, you're being fed to wolves that are interested only in how they can use you financially. You are being instructed and manipulated by perverted Hollywood producers and directors who trade sex for favors, globalized corporations that care only about profit and extracting your labor, corrupt politicians who will say anything to increase their power, CEOs of social networking companies who design their products to be harmful and addictive, and media outlets that preach equality to the point of destroying the idea that there are two biological sexes.

These forces have removed or minimized the most positive influence in your life, a good husband, and replaced it with brainwashing that normalizes toxic behaviors that feed your devil. Since you were young, you've been incessantly bombarded with messages that starve your angel, leading you down the wrong path.

With women firmly under control, and the universities and media pushing feminism, men can also be controlled. Men are reactive in that they respond to the signals women put out. If women signal that they want status and excitement, men will give them those things to get sex and intimacy. On the other hand, if women signal that they value virtue and motherhood, men will be inclined to feed their angel and pursue having a family.

When a masculine man meets you, he picks up signals that indicate who you are and what you want before putting you in a "wife" box or "promiscuous" box. A woman who sends messages that she is a feminist will be put in the promiscuous box, and it may be something as subtle as you saying that your career is "important." A man will then seek only sex or a non-committed relationship with you. Men who understand the nature of women want to settle down with one who leans traditional, not feminist.

If both men and women are feeding their devils, families are not created. The elites prefer this because a nation of strong families is hard to control, whereas a nation of sex-obsessed bonobos who care only about themselves and their genitals can be easily steered like a car. Society weakens if it concentrates on fame, money, sex, and consumer products to achieve fulfillment instead of love, family, and God.

Another damaging feature of feminism is that it has made it easy for women to terminate their families through divorce laws. You already know that if your husband makes more money than you and you divorce him, you're set to earn monthly alimony payments on top of taking the home. If children are involved, you also know it's highly likely that the judge will grant you custody, even if you've displayed signs that you are less fit than the father. Your devil is well-versed in the law and will encourage you to dump your husband for a more exciting prospect or lifestyle, even if your husband is fulfilling his role as a provider. Many women even make false accusations of domestic violence to ensure that the courts will rule in their favor.

I know many men who are avoiding marriage solely because of divorce laws. They believe it is unjust that their lives can be turned upside down emotionally and financially because a woman decided that she is bored with being married. Many women celebrated when divorce laws were rewritten in their favor, but now that the consequences of these laws are apparent, men are swearing off marriage altogether or going to foreign countries with a less punitive legal system. How do pro-woman divorce laws help women if fewer men are willing to marry them?

Considering the hostility towards marriage and family life, it's no surprise that men pursue casual relationships. In terms of their self-preservation, it is the logical choice, but these men suffer in the end because they never create a family. Men resent women for not being more virtuous, loyal, and wifely, while women resent men for not committing to them. Both remain divided and miserable. In the meantime, politicians and the disseminators of culture push the sexes further apart to enrich themselves by keeping women enslaved in careers while advancing a perverted anti-family agenda where they promote transsexuality and homosexual marriage instead of heterosexual marriage.

Unless you're skilled at identifying the subtle feminist messages in TV shows, movies, news articles, pop songs, and advertisements, you will allow them to gradually program how you think until you accept the feminist view of the world as normal. You're also being influenced by your friends. It's been said that a man or woman is the product of their four or five closest friends. If these friends are feminists, doomed to being single, they will sabotage your efforts to create a family, because they want you to be as lonely as they are. Who else would they complain to about how hard it is to be a woman if you succeed at finding a husband who dedicates himself to you? Many people act like crabs in a bucket, where if one crab attempts to escape, the other crabs pull it down. With an ideology like feminism, this is almost always the case.

I know that I can't single-handedly fight all the feminist influences in the environment that are programming a girlfriend of mine to feed her devil, so I try to find a girl who has some intrinsic resistance to the poison, such as being raised by religious parents who emphasized traditional values. Otherwise, it's me against the world, and this is a fight I cannot win. The fact that you're even reading this book shows that you undoubtedly have a natural resistance to feminism.

Finding Yourself

Many women think that if they have a large number of exciting experiences, especially with men, they will know who they "really" are. Instead, these experiences will take them away from having a family and signal to men that they're not worth a long-term relationship.

Once you have what you need to survive and live in basic comfort, anything you pursue apart from family is feeding your devil. He wants you to pursue good-looking and famous men in exotic lands so that you'll feel excited. He wants you to sample the finest foods, designer clothing, and luxuries so that you'll get a dopamine rush from experiencing new pleasures. He wants you to pursue a career and watch the numbers in your bank account grow so that you'll feel like a success. The harder you pursue these goals, the more you will be taken away from having a family. The type of man who is ready for marriage doesn't want to marry a woman who is running on the treadmill of materialism unless he is also running on that same treadmill.

Pursuits outside of family will simply lead to failed relationships as you demand an ever-higher standard of men, which will make it much harder for you to connect with a man in the future. Even worse, you waste valuable time while your biological clock is ticking and your beauty, the main piece of bait that God has given you to land a man, declines. If you're single and over 30, the risk that you will not get married is greater than it was when you were in your early twenties because your fertility is decreasing, your beauty is fading, and your standards are rising. The older a woman, the lower her standards should be if she wants to get married, but the opposite tends to occur.

By now, I hope you can see the crime of forcing women to pursue an education and career before having a family. Women have different biological clocks than men and should not be on the same educational and career timelines. If I had my way, women would focus on creating a family straight after finishing high school and attend university only once their last child is in school. This would ensure that they don't miss out on having a family from making a career their priority.

Men have more time to find themselves, because in the eyes of most women, their value doesn't peak until their mid-thirties, but in the eyes of the best men, a woman's value tends to peak in her early twenties, which in modern society is when few women are actively trying to land a husband.

I'm 39 and single after spending years "finding myself" by traveling the world, yet I can still go into a nightclub and land girls in their early twenties. A woman who is 39 can attract men who want to sleep with her, but she will find it far harder to attract a good man who wants to *commit* to her, because the material prizes she has accumulated since she was in her early twenties (money, credentials, trips to exotic locations, a fancy job title) are less valuable to men than beauty.

While men will want to have sex with you even if you're fifty or older, they will be most willing to marry you when your beauty is at its peak and you're not as jaded or masculinized from a corporate career and numerous sexual experiences. You can argue that it is sad for a man of my age to judge women mainly by their youth, innocence, and beauty, but this is how men were created. You should use this fact to your advantage instead of letting it upset you.

A journey to find oneself is more likely to be fruitful for a man than a woman. A man usually—but not always—processes his experiences through a filter of logic in order to connect the dots of his existence and learn how to be more attractive to women. A woman, through no fault of her own, processes her experiences through a filter of emotion to increase her pleasure or self-validation, without attempting to put these experiences in context. The more experience a man has, the more likely he will get what he wants in the future, but the more experience a woman has, the less likely she will get what she wants in the future.

For example, a woman finds it difficult to accept that every sexy man she sleeps with makes it harder for her to fall in love with a good man in the future, particularly one who could become her husband. The more sexual experiences a woman has, the less likely she will be happy *at all*, because she will spend her life trying to relive the "fun" years, which had more to do with her being at the peak of her youth and beauty than her inherent abilities or intelligence. If a woman listens to her devil, she will experience an emotional high from being sexually desired in her late teens and early twenties, and then spend the rest of her life in a futile quest to duplicate this high, skipping over "boring" good men along the way. You therefore have far more to lose through experience than a man.

Also, consider that it's easier for men to embark on a journey that is completely independent of women. The fact that there is a tradition of monasteries and Eastern asceticism, with men forgoing women entirely to become monks, with far fewer women becoming nuns, is a clue that it's easier for a man to decide not to be with women and move to a cabin in the woods with only furry animals to keep him company. Men greatly desire women, but they need them less than you need a man.

It's tougher for you to be alone because your nature demands that you attach your identity to either family or God. When a man sets out on a personal journey to find himself, he may kill several men in battle, discover the truths of the universe, or become spiritually enlightened. When a woman sets out on a journey to find herself, she gets pumped and dumped by a dozen men, becomes a manager in an office, or buys a cat or two. For women, there is no pot of gold at the end of a rainbow of experience. It should not be your goal.

Accept that it's okay to depend on a man and exist through him, because in exchange for that you achieve the love that you cannot without him. Find a man who loves you and take him with you on your life's journey, but going it alone in the hope that you will learn something new or become a more experienced woman will just make it harder—if not impossible—for you to find a man at all.

If you decide to find yourself by feeding your devil, you will waste thousands of hours dating and being used like a sex doll. Then you'll spend thousands of more hours with your girlfriends *talking* about dating and how you were used like a sex doll. You'll gradually develop a subtle hatred towards men for not choosing to wife you up even though you never put out wifely signals to them.

I know I'm an outlier, but do you want to guess how much time I've spent learning game and pursuing women? I used to go out four nights a week to chase them, treating it like a job. I've been to more than twenty countries with the aim of learning about the local women and how to seduce them. I've written fourteen books and counting dedicated to explaining my pickup tactics. I've talked to thousands of women, gone on hundreds of dates, and slept with so many women that I've forgotten most of my conquests.

My sexual experiences have given me the wisdom and knowledge to have a career as a writer, but I don't have anyone to love or a family of my own. If I could get in a time machine, go back to when I graduated from college, and ask my Iranian father to arrange a marriage with a girl from his country, I would not be an atomized man writing this book in a hipster café as I am now. I would have teenage children, a wife, and an army of pugs. Perhaps I'd have less money, and undoubtedly I would be less famous, but the emptiness I feel would be filled.

Like me, there are many women who are single and in their late thirties, but because men are attracted to beauty and women to status, which I possess some of, I have a higher chance than a woman my age of creating a positive outcome. It's unfortunate that feminism is teaching women to live according to the male biological clock by pursuing fun, career, and other ego-based goals before family. These women will continue to suffer as long as they attempt to find themselves through experiences instead of finding one good man who will love them.

Strong And Independent

"He can't handle a strong, successful, intelligent, powerful woman." When a girl is rejected by a man, she preserves her ego and relieves the pain of rejection by bragging about the traits she thinks she has, but these traits are almost always what men don't want in a woman. Her declaration of strength is like a young boy flexing his muscles to show how strong he is. That may be a cute display, but it's not a demonstration of genuine strength. A woman can never be strong in the same way as a man, who would ultimately kill other human beings to protect his family.

Are you ready to murder others to keep your family, husband, children, and friends safe? Probably not, but I am, and this is why I have identified a number of potential weapons in the different rooms of my home that can kill or maim. The aggression and "toxic masculinity" that feminists love to complain about today are what kept women alive in the past, and which continue to keep them safe through the male-dominated fields of military and law enforcement. If this barbarism were switched off entirely, men would lose their innate ability to protect their families and morph into gay best friends, whom few women would want to marry.

While a woman can possess other forms of strength, it is nearly impossible for them to exceed the innate barbaric strength of the average man, even if they have undergone specialized combat training. This is not to say that you are inferior to men, since you possess many traits that men don't have, but strength in life-or-death situations is not one of them. When something goes drastically wrong, women often resort to crying as a bat signal that they want help, a strategy that is quite effective because it consistently elicits sympathy from masculine men.

Where did women get the idea that men crave "strong" women? Ever since you were a toddler, you were taught in schools, by television, and through other cultural messages that men and women are literally equal from the neck up. As a result, you may have come to believe that whatever you're attracted to, a man must also be attracted to. What are women attracted to? Status, intelligence, strength, confidence, money, and power. What do many women *think* men are attracted to? Status, intelligence, strength, confidence, money, and power. But what are men *really* attracted to? Beauty, femininity, and loyalty.

A woman who thinks that men are attracted to the same things as she is will be the first to fail in the marriage game, because she'll insist on displaying qualities that masculine men don't want for long-term relationships. It's certainly a bonus if my future wife can bring in some income, and I wouldn't mind her being intelligent enough to handle a deep conversation with me, but her desire to put family above career is ten times more important than any second-ary trait that is not essential to creating a family.

You need only enough strength and independence to find a man who possesses genuine strength and independ-ence. This means that you should pursue employment that merely allows you to maintain your beauty and ensure you have what you need to survive. Beyond this, you're expending your time and energy on things that won't increase your chances of landing a good man. The more you become caught up in your career, the more you'll convince yourself that it's the most important part of your life. It then becomes inevitable that you will pursue exciting sexual encounters to compensate for your soul-destroying office job while your biological clock steadily ticks away.

Ask any woman whose long-term relationship fell apart around the age of 30 and you'll sense her panic. I had a relationship end when I was 37, and though I was deeply upset, I didn't feel panicked, because my father had his last child when he was in his early fifties. Although not ideal, it's entirely possible for me to take a few years off, start hunting for a wife when I am in my early forties, and start a family *a decade later*. A woman can't do this unless she pays vast sums of money for fertility treatments that are not guaranteed to succeed.

The reason men work is so they are seen as attractive mates. It's not because they love being stuck in an office for forty hours a week—they innately know that women don't want a man who is poor. They work because they *have* to work. On the other hand, women start working at a young age because they are programmed to do so after being sold a false bill of goods that a career will be more fulfilling than having a family. Once your career satisfies all of your basic needs, and you no longer need a man to provide for you, your devil will tell you to seek high-status men. The problem is that many women confuse high-status men with men who don't care about them, which ensures that they will end up in bad relationships that don't lead to marriage.

Having a career enables you to effortlessly feed your devil. If your financial status were much lower, and you genuinely needed a stable man in order to lead a comfortable life, would you pay any attention to a starving artist or musician? Would you be impressed by the "bad boy" drug dealer who you know has a rotation of other women? Would you quickly sleep with the alpha Chad who simply invites you over for sex without putting in any effort? The more stable and successful your career, the more likely you will seek relationships with men who won't commit to you.

Nice guys are now deliberately acting like jerks, "fuck-boys," and assholes because it's the best way for them to get laid. I teach men how to simulate alpha-male behavior because women no longer want providers. When a man shows you his business card in the hope of impressing you, he is executing a game that worked for his grandfather in the days when few women worked, but today's woman doesn't need a man's money—she needs a tall man with big muscles and flawless facial aesthetics who makes her feel butterflies in her stomach by paying her backhanded compliments and not showing too much interest.

The more stable and comfortable you are financially, the more you will gravitate towards seeking men who excite you. You must consciously block this pattern of behavior by ignoring your devil's call to seek an alpha male or "bad boy" who you think has high status. If you don't, you're in danger of losing your chance at creating a family.

Another sign that your job isn't essential for a healthy marriage is to ask what would happen if you lost your job and couldn't get another one. Would your husband leave you? It's extremely unlikely. I've never heard of a case where a man left his wife because she was unemployed. Now let's consider the opposite scenario, where a man loses his job and remains unemployed. Will his wife leave him? Not only will she leave him, but we can expect that she will do so within two years.

This shows that men don't value a woman who has a job nearly as much as a woman values a man who has one. If you do find a man who claims that his future wife's employment is important, it's because he has been pro-grammed to believe in the cult of equality and is insufficiently masculine to take pride in being able to take care of his family on his own. It's unlikely that you will be deeply attracted to this type of man, or you won't feel completely confident that he will be able to protect and provide for the family, which increases the likelihood that you will cheat on him.

One great thing about being a woman is that if you find a successful man, you have the option of not working. Men never have this option. Unless a man finds a career that allows him to wake up whenever he wants and set his own schedule (as I can), he will slowly destroy his soul in an office job, where he stares at a computer screen for dozens of hours a week while enduring petty politics, mind-numbing meetings, and extended periods of sitting that slowly degrade his muscles, leading to chronic back and neck pain. His income may be high, and he may be able to afford the best of what a "Made in China" materialist life can offer, but if a man takes materialism too far and does not focus on creating a family, he will resort to over-eating, alcohol abuse, drugs, video games, pornography, meaning-less sex, or some other hollow vice. It's not only women who are affected by the ills of modern society.

The bottom line is that you will not find lasting fulfill-ment through a career. It's a wretched dead end. Many books have been written on how to find happiness by pursuing a career, but that approach leads to failure, and the latest trend of finding a "work-life" balance will also fail, because it's impossible to contort female nature to that of a man's, who, unlike a woman, *must* work in order to signal to his potential wife that he can provide for her. Women who are seeking providers will always appreciate men with a career, but a man seeking the future mother of his children is far less likely to.

A shortcut to knowing that a man is serious about creat-ing a family is if he doesn't seem to care about your career. The more a man peppers you with questions about your "five-year plan" or path to middle management, as if he were conducting a job interview, the more likely he's stuck on the materialist treadmill and is less concerned about family than money.

When I'm on a date with a girl, I ask about her job to find out the extent to which she is entrenched in a masculine-oriented career program. If she says "lawyer," "doctor," or "marketing manager," I know she will be so committed to her career that she will forsake having a family until her thirties. On the other hand, I jump for joy when I find out she has a menial job, such as supermarket clerk, because there's no way she will sacrifice a family for that. For this reason, I actively pursue cute women who work in supermarkets.

A second question I ask a date is when she wants to have children. Unless she says in two or three years' time and tells me something that shows she's excited at the prospect of becoming a mother, I know she's not serious about having a family and hasn't put as much thought into it as she has into making money. Understand that a man who is serious about having a family has ways to uncover your intentions based on what you say. If you want to turn off family-orientated men and select for ones who want only sex, there is no better way to do so than by saying you are a career woman who is "not interested in children yet." He will immediately place you in the pump-and-dump category.

Instead of asking how you can find fulfillment through a career, it's better to ask how holding down a basic job will enable you to find fulfillment through a good man with whom you can establish a family. If you leave your parents' home, you're essentially forcing yourself to have a career so that you can pay for the high cost of enjoying a *Sex and the City* lifestyle. A better solution is to live with your parents so that you can devote more of your energy to finding a husband instead of wasting it on the rat race. Your parents are unlikely to mind you living at home, and doing so makes it harder for you to feed your devil through casual sex. It's so easy to have sex while living alone that I've told men to assume that a woman has at least three new sexual partners for every year she has lived on her own. It won't take long for her ability to form a pair-bond with a good man to be irreversibly damaged.

When I wanted only sex from girls, I deliberately filtered out the ones who lived with their parents, because they were much harder to sleep with. Now, I am unable to contain my excitement when I meet a girl who lives at home and has to check in with mom by sending a text message stating she'll be home soon. While you may think that I'm the exception in how I judge girls by their family values, there is a reactionary trend among men against women who have a feminist lifestyle.

The fact that you're even reading this book, written by a man who has been deplatformed and attacked in thousands of media articles, and are gaining value from it in spite of being taught anti-traditional ideas for many years, is an indication of the shift to a light form of traditionalism. Every year, thousands of women are waking up to the fact that careers and casual sex prevent them from forming a family. At the same time, men are becoming wise to not marry women who have a history of promiscuous behavior. I won't be surprised if a man you go on a date with in the future brings up this very book as a way to test whether you have traditional beliefs.

In the end, a woman who is seriously committed to her career is more likely to neglect her family than a woman who is not, because the former is dedicating at least 35% of her waking hours to something that doesn't increase love in the home. *"But I have to work, or else we can't meet basic expenses!"* There is a sliver of truth to this argument, especially if you live in an expensive city such as the one I come from (Washington, D.C.), but it's likely your financial goals far exceed the need to survive, and revolve around a bigger house, fine dining, and luxury vehicles. If a housewife can sew, garden, cook, and homeschool, there will be little need for her to work. The expenses saved on daycare and automobiles, combined with a frugal lifestyle and the possibility of homeschooling, will be more than enough to make a single-income household viable.

Single-income households won't have a lavish lifestyle, but they will be full of meaning because the mother can spend much more time at home instead of devoting her energy to pleasing the demands of a corporate boss while her children are raised by strangers making close to minimum wage. Tales of abuse in day-care centers are enough for me to insist that my children never step foot in one. I find it unfortunate that so many women go against their maternal instincts and leave their children with strangers for most of the day during their most crucial years of development.

Is it possible to have both a successful career and a happy family? Unless you're a millionaire and can hire an army of assistants and nannies, such as *Lean In* author and Facebook executive Sheryl Sandberg, the answer is no. A typical middle-class woman will not be able to live the feminist dream of pursuing a high-powered career while raising a family. It cuts her nature in two, causing intense inner conflict and dissatisfaction. At work, she is forced to feed her devil, compete like a man, and pursue materialist gains for the sake of money, while at home she is expected to listen to her angel and be a nurturing mother who also wants to please her husband. This doesn't work in practice. What ends up happening is that she stays in work mode at home, makes demands on her husband as if he were a co-worker, and treats her children like a business project to be managed, and this is assuming she has any energy left after a full day at the office.

My mother raised me and my younger sister after she divorced my dad when I was nine years old. Even though she came home exhausted from her physically demanding job as a seamstress, she cooked us a meal and cleaned the house while I watched TV or played video games. As a result, she yelled at me countless times for being ungrateful and not helping around the house. Having a full-time job *and* taking care of the home often sent her over the emotional edge. We bickered regularly because of it. Our relationship was strained for many years, especially when I was in my late teens. After she retired, our relationship became stronger, because she wasn't draining herself and—perhaps justifiably—taking out her frustrations on me.

I learned from my mother that it's too much for a woman to work full-time and take care of the home. Even if you're able to pull it off, as my mom did, it puts a huge strain on family relationships and makes your life overly stressful. Since raising a family is a full-time job of its own, it's simply not fair to expect a woman to also work outside the home.

To accommodate women having their own careers, the culture tells husbands to pick up the slack and become something like a Mr. Mom by helping out with the chores. This only makes the problem worse, because it takes your man away from the role you want to see him in—a strong leader—and turns him more into a woman. I have read a dubious study that men who do more household chores get less sex from their wives. Whether or not this is true, it's easy to see why a woman would not want to sleep with a man who acts like an equal partner or a gay best friend instead of a masculine leader.

The ideal scenario is for the husband to work hard to provide for his family during the day and relax with his wife and children in the evening. While he's at work, the wife takes care of the home, runs errands, and prepares dinner. This is far more superior to the schizophrenic model we have now where both parents work and the children are dumped in daycare or come home from school to an empty house, only to spend time with a stressed-out mom and dad who are staring at their smartphones.

I deem it impossible for a woman to have a career and a family at the same time. It will create too much stress, forcing her to feed her devil while starving her angel. There are exceptions, such as if a woman has a part-time job, works from home, or is exceedingly rich, but the standard model of educating a woman for four years in university, when she's at the peak of her fertility, then pushing her to spend several more years working on her career instead of establishing herself with a good man, and then continuing to work in that career after a late marriage, thereby sacrificing her family and increasing the likelihood of divorce, is untenable. You should not tolerate or accept it, because it goes against your female nature or feeds its most negative side.

You may be afraid of what will happen if you marry a man who cheats, becomes abusive, or turns into an alcoholic when you don't have a career. If you have to leave him but don't have any job skills, what will you do to survive? First, every Western nation has welfare for single mothers. You won't become destitute or homeless, even if you have no family or friends to help you.

Secondly, the likelihood of this happening is low if you resist the urge to select a "bad boy" who has shown signs of substance abuse, violent behavior, dishonesty, or philandering. If you feed your devil when selecting a man, he will provide you with a devilish outcome. While there are cases where a good man turns bad over the years, it's more common for the warning signs to be present early in the relationship. We no longer live in an age where you are expected to marry a man chosen for you by your family, so you must take full responsibility for your choice in men. If you let notions of a Hollywood-style whirlwind romance guide your decisions, things will end in disaster.

The third reason you should not worry about destitution is that divorce laws are so rigged in your favor that it's more likely your ex-husband will be put in jail for not paying child or spousal support than you going homeless. These divorce laws need to change because they're unfair to men and discourage them from getting married in the first place, which reduces your pool of potential husbands.

If you select for the good man who wants to protect and provide, you will greatly minimize the risk of marrying a bad man, though of course there are no guarantees in marriage. Life has a way of surprising us, and sometimes we must take the good with the bad. The main point is not to let old wives' tales of husbands going bad push you into choosing a career over a family. This was a far bigger problem in the past when there was no government welfare, no domestic violence laws, and a woman didn't have complete freedom to choose whom she wanted to marry.

Once you accept that pursuing a career takes you away from your goal of establishing and maintaining a family, the question arises whether it's even worthwhile for any woman to go to university.

University Education

In the past, it wasn't necessary for a wife to have more than a middle school or high school education, because her husband would have a useful skill and work until his back gave out. Now, according to feminist ideology, women who choose to be housewives are "slaves," while women who choose a career are superheroes. To make men accept this change, they had to be relentlessly emasculated until they saw women as an equally masculine partner, but this has so greatly weakened men that women no longer trust them to be strong enough to lead, perpetuating a cycle where a woman may feel she has no choice but to pursue a career if she wants to be materially secure.

Today, men and women compete for jobs and riches, putting family on the backburner. During this pursuit of "success," they seek harmful pleasures by feeding their devils, who have no trouble tempting fatigued and confused souls. Casual sex becomes a habit, making you so narcissistic, entitled, and damaged that you can never properly bond with a potential spouse.

Hookup culture, which often starts in high school, has trained men to believe that sex is no big deal and should happen no later than the third date, and in some cases no later than the third hour upon meeting a new female. With millions of empowered women giving up their vaginas on the flimsiest of impulses, most men (including the good ones) don't want to wait for sex. This means that even if you go the traditional route of avoiding university and a career to focus on having a family, your odds of success will increase only marginally because most men will not value your traditional outlook. The man who wants a family will certainly value it, but even the bulk of my male readers, who are far more traditionally minded than average, are so distrustful of women and the existing system that they may pass on marriage and choose something that resembles co-habitation instead. So what's a good woman to do?

First, let's describe what happens to a typical 18-year-old girl who goes to university today. She will spend four years racking up tens of thousands of dollars in debt for a degree that is likely to be in the humanities or social sciences. She will be immersed in an environment that promotes hooking up with men who are "hot," "sexy," or "popular." She will spend hundreds of hours studying and reading books, but zero hours becoming a good wife from learning basic cooking or homemaking skills. No matter what she majors in, she will be indoctrinated in feminism and embrace the belief that men are the enemy, pushing family down her list of priorities. And she will consume copious amounts of junk food, alcohol, and maybe drugs.

Some women have been able to resist the temptations of a university environment, but it's safe to say that most emerge from the experience spiritually poorer, less in tune with their feminine nature, more committed to securing a career, more in debt thanks to student loans, and less likely to get married within five years. For every story you hear of college sweethearts getting married, you hear dozens more of a woman who dyed her hair green, got her first tattoo, experienced a threesome, and got pumped and dumped by multiple Chads. Unless a woman goes to college specifically with the aim of meeting a potential husband, the outcome will be negative.

It's important to consider how a student loan impacts your ability to land a husband. The law is complicated in this area. Usually, your husband isn't legally obligated for the debts you sustained before marrying him, but your repayments will have an effect on his finances and the household budget. Most men will regard your debt as their own if you get married, and if you have a lot of debt, they will be more inclined to stay away.

The situation is more dire if you have a large amount of student loan debt *and* a low-paying job, because it's likely that you won't ever be able to pay it off. The burden will almost certainly fall on your potential husband, who will take your debt into account when deciding whether or not you're worth a long-term commitment. If you're perfect in every other way, the debt may not affect his decision, but if you have few other black marks on your record, such as a history of promiscuous behavior, he may decide to walk away. Having student loan debt that is under control will show a man that it will not be a burden to him.

Once you realize the damaging consequences of pursuing career, I recommend the drastic option of not going to university at all. In modern culture, this seems totally out of the question, because it's assumed that a university education is essential for a useful career, but this career may come at the cost of never getting married. You end up cash-rich but family poor. We have to tread a middle path between these two extremes and view education not from the perspective of how much money it will enable you to earn in the future, but how it will help you to find a husband and be content within marriage.

Which option will allow you to take care of your basic needs and find a good man without having to endure the degeneracy and ideological programming of the university environment, which urges you to see men as the enemy and your career as some sort of salvation? Depending on your age and circumstances, the best option is likely skipping university and working in simple jobs where you will come into contact with potential husbands who find your traditional values highly attractive. Or it may be to enroll in a community college with low tuition fees and dabbling in courses out of intellectual curiosity. Or it may be to attend a four-year university that is cheap, doesn't burden you with debt, and where you study practical (science-based) subjects instead of those steeped in anti-family ideology.

Let's imagine that you skip university and become a low-paying assistant in a predominately male office. One of these men with a promising future falls in love with you and proposes marriage. You get married at the age of 22 and become pregnant a year later. It is assumed that once you have the baby, you will quit your job, which doesn't bring in much income anyway. As your child grows up, you will have more time to focus on your hobbies. And then you get pregnant again.

You and your husband decide that two children are enough. Eventually, both of them will be in elementary school. You'll now have more free time because when the kids come home from school, they won't need constant attention and care as was the case when they were younger. This is when it makes sense for you to pursue higher education if you still want to. While your children are at school, you are free to go to school part-time, assuming it doesn't conflict with your household duties. When they become young adults and go to university, you have the option of easing into a full-time career. Yes, your female co-workers will be ahead of you on the corporate ladder, and you will start at a lower pay grade, but you will have something they won't: grown-up children.

This is just one possible scenario that suggests it makes sense for a woman to educate herself after she has children instead of before. Life is long, and if you're 45 and have an empty nest, you still have at least three *decades* in which to pursue other interests. This is more than enough time to start a career or a business, provided it doesn't harm your family.

If I have the opportunity to create a family, I would like to have at least four children. This will ensure that my wife will never become "bored" or idle, because many modern technological appliances make child-rearing less difficult than in the past. If she does get bored at some point, she will have the option of working while the children are occupied with their education, assuming we don't home-school.

If you would like a career at some point, you can have it, because there is no biological clock stopping you from working at 60 or later, but there definitely is a biological clock that prevents you from having children after 40. First take care of the clock that ticks faster. Men and women have different biological clocks, so I hope you see the absurdity of putting both on the same university and career timeline, which was originally developed for men, not women.

Ideally, the culture should encourage only men to go to university so women can focus on starting a family at an age that is in line with their biological clock. I know most women will regard this as too radical. They will say it's not fair for them to stay at home, thinking that it's easy or fun for a husband to be the sole provider when it actually comes with huge amounts of responsibility. As a man, I'm ready to take on this responsibility, assuming my wife accepts her share of the bargain and provides my brood with a proper home. I would rather my family live in somewhat impoverished conditions with a dedicated wife than in wealth with a semi-absent wife who didn't devote her time to the family.

With much of the theory out of the way, I can now proceed with the more practical matter of how to find a man.

Book II: Men

Bad Boys

Many women are attracted to bad boys who can never become suitable husbands. Once you understand why this is part of your nature, the problem won't be difficult to solve.

First, remember that there is a positive and a negative side to your nature. Your angel focuses on nurturing and love, while your devil focuses on limitless materialism and scoring high-status men. When your devil is in control, which is the case for most women, you mistake the character of a bad boy, jerk, or asshole with having "high status," whereas he is low status in terms of being a good husband. You assume that a man who doesn't care about you has high status simply because he doesn't care about you.

Women have no clear way to judge the status of men. They're not a computer that can process the hundreds of different variables that make up a man's essence and spit out a value that tells them whether or not they should proceed with a relationship. Instead, they look for shortcuts, and the two most common shortcuts are if other women like a man and if a man treats them badly.

If other women like a man, you assume that these women have done the hard work of judging his value and that you can automatically like him without having to judge him yourself. If he doesn't treat you well, you assume that you must be beneath him in some way, because if his value was lower than yours, he would treat you like a princess and do all sorts of favors for you. You see a famous musician or actor as high status not necessarily because he is talented, but because so many other women give him positive attention. You see the tattooed playboy as high status because he treats you like dirt. This is even more the case if other women like him *and* he treats you poorly, because you will incorrectly think he's your one-in-a-billion soulmate.

Needless to say, these shortcuts do not work in finding a husband. They will cause you to become attached to a player who is enjoying a buffet of sexual options, or a deadbeat who will not stick around as a provider and protector. In a society that feeds only your devil, you use these two shortcuts to pick men who will merely provide you with entertaining sex.

It gets even worse: having a career (or collecting government welfare) provides you with an income that results in seeing a man's ability to provide as *low* value while you are in the prime of your beauty. Instead, you place greater emphasis on his looks, height, banter, humor, and sexiness. When a provider tries to please you, you put him on the backburner, because such a man doesn't feed your devil.

In my game books for men, I teach them how to hijack the two shortcuts. The first way is through "social proof," where I tell men how they can signal to a woman that they are on friendly terms with other attractive women. When I'm in a club, it's to my advantage if women see another beautiful woman touching me and flirting with me, because they will think that she has deemed my value to be high. In my early game days, I would stage pictures of myself with hot women, knowing that other women would see them, which enabled me to get more notches.

My second piece of advice for men is not to be nice. In other words, don't act like a provider and protector, because most women are feeding their devil and want men who have status or provide excitement. The best way for men to do this is to treat a woman badly by being aloof and teasing them. A man who is nice will win a woman's heart if she is Mormon, Amish, or otherwise highly religious, but if she is not, he will repel her. For a man to at least get sex in the modern era, he must provide women with the status, excitement, drama, and physical attraction they crave.

Men who follow my advice will get laid, but sadly they may not get any closer to a relationship that leads to marriage, because they ultimately do not want to marry a woman who succumbs to social proof and bad boy behavior. Such a woman is more likely to jump ship for another man who displays even higher status. The fact that men have to put in so much work just for sex, with little chance of enjoying a meaningful relationship, is why so many of them are dropping out of the game entirely.

Sex is an important need for men, and I try to give them advice that is powerful enough to work on at least a physical level, but the mating game has become a dismal proposition for males. It's easy for a man to chase women when he's at the peak of his horniness, but once that tapers off, his subconscious tells him there is nothing more he can gain from women than cheap sex. In other words, if you're wondering why a potential date isn't calling you back or putting in the work to seduce you, it's because his rewards from doing so in his past were non-existent. You'll have to combat this by signaling that he will indeed be rewarded if he pursues you.

Men who are in the dating game today have the knowledge and tools to trick you easily. I know how to front-load all the cool things about me when I first meet a girl to trigger an explosion of status in her mind. I even know how to be just vague enough when I answer her questions to spike her curiosity further. Your ability to judge a man can be so deficient that it's possible for one to play video games all day and not have any real-life experience but still make you think he's a worthwhile hookup. It's too much of a risk for you to choose your male partners on emotion or gut instinct alone.

If you were born in Europe, America, Canada, or Australia, you were raised in an environment that trained you to forsake your angel and feed your devil. Just being able to read English enables me to confirm that treating you badly, or at least showing that I don't care about you, will excite you enough to start giving me the attention I need to fornicate with you. I've done it too many times to count, and have taught tens of thousands of men around the world to do the same.

Even though I've shared a few game tricks with you, you'll still fall for them until you make a conscious effort to starve your devil and stop pursuing the reward of sex with an exciting, high-status man. What you may think of as listening to your instincts is really your devil feeding you harmful instructions. Trusting your instincts when your angel is absent will result in pursuing men who do not commit to you, and this pattern will continue for decades until the type of man you prefer no longer finds you attractive.

The first step to breaking this cycle and making better decisions is to overlay your malformed instincts with logic. With every man you meet, when the time comes to decide whether or not to take the interaction to a more intimate level, ask yourself the following: **"Is this the type of man who will provide and protect?"** If the answer is no, you should not go any further unless you don't mind getting pumped and dumped.

A man who is not ready to provide or protect is feeding his own devil, which means he pursues sex for pleasure, variety, novelty, ego gratification, and excitement, and once these benefits disappear, which they usually do in a matter of weeks, he will bail on you without feeling any guilt. As I'm sure you already know, you cannot turn a player into a husband by convincing or persuading him to starve his devil. He must make the personal decision to listen to his angel *before* he meets you. This means that what you see is what you get. Apart from some superficial aspects, such as a man's hairstyle or clothing, you will not change the essence of who a man is. If he changes a significant aspect of who he is, it will be because *he* made a conscious decision to change and not because of your influence.

Let's say that you're in a nightclub with your friends for a birthday party. Out of the corner of your eye, you notice a man talking to a beautiful woman who seems to be engaged in the conversation. He is stylish and one of the most attractive men in the room. He eventually walks up to you and introduces himself as Eric.

Eric's conversation is smooth, and next thing you know you're at the bar with him while he orders a drink from a bartender who knows his name. You can't help but giggle at his jokes. He then cuts the conversation short and asks for your number while another beautiful woman seems eager to talk to him. Should you give him your number?

Let's ask our logical question: "Is this the type of man who will provide and protect?" This is an easy no. A man doesn't work on his game and hit the nightlife in order to get married and settle down, especially if he's getting attention from many beautiful women. This man will give you excitement but nothing more, and you won't be able to hold his attention for long even if you're beautiful yourself because commitment with one beautiful girl is not what his devil wants.

Now imagine you're in a crowded café reading a book. An average-looking man who desperately needs a style makeover asks whether he can share your table. As you're getting ready to leave, he asks what kind of book you're reading and if you like it. You notice that perspiration is forming on his forehead. You politely respond to him, and he does his best to maintain the conversation, but there are many awkward silences. He introduces himself as Bobby.

You are not immediately attracted to Bobby, but he seems to be a nice man with some redeeming qualities and a stable job. He finally asks for your number. Should you give it to him? To help you decide, realize that men who are not smooth around women find it very time-consuming and laborious to find just one woman to date. They prefer to focus on work, hobbies, sports, or socializing with friends. Because of this, they will avoid pumping and dumping a girl they're interested in since it takes too much effort to find another girl, causing them to focus more on relationships than casual sex. Therefore, Bobby is a far better candidate than Eric to provide and protect.

On one extreme we have Exciting Eric and on the other we have Boring Bobby. Most of your encounters with men will fall somewhere in between. The problem is that your devil prefers Exciting Eric, who is ideal for one night only. It is likely that there have been many Boring Bobbies in your life who you put in the friend zone for safekeeping until the day when you could no longer get the attention of an Exciting Eric, but the problem with this strategy is that Boring Bobby will eventually find a girl who recognizes his worth.

You may argue that Bobby doesn't give you "butter-flies." There isn't any "chemistry." He doesn't have any "interesting" hobbies. He's not "spontaneous" enough. He lacks "confidence." All these complaints are from your devil, which wants you to find a man who can give you a temporary emotional high. If you insist on chasing emotional highs, it will be impossible for commitment to blossom.

Men will have sex with a girl they don't care about simply to experience an orgasm or two, but they will only commit to a girl they believe has genuine worth. If you've been pumped and dumped, it means you were pursuing men who either weren't looking to provide and protect or who wanted a relationship with a girl whose value was higher than yours. Remember that you want to find a man who sees your value as so high that he thinks he can't get any better. From your devil's perspective, it will be with a man who doesn't seem like the best you can get. In other words, if your devil likes a man, beware! Your devil will always push you towards someone who will not provide and protect for what should be the rest of your life.

I can guarantee that your devil is in revolt right now. He wants you to reject my advice and focus on gaining the attention of Exciting Eric. *"Roosh doesn't know what he's talking about! He's trying to sabotage our efforts! He wants us to have a boring life! And his beard is ugly!"* You already know what happens if you trust your devil: failure to create a family. Boring Bobby will treat you well and not feed his own devil by becoming a cheater, and what he lacks in excitement will be more than compensated with a lasting love that is similar to what your grandparents experienced. Consider that by giving you this advice, I'm cockblocking myself, because the vibe I put out is more exciting than boring. If every woman in the world followed what I'm sharing right now, my casual sex life and that of my male followers would suffer greatly, but it would undoubtedly result in healthier relationships for everyone.

Even though I'm spelling out what you need to do, you will find it tough to resist an Exciting Eric in the future. When he sends you a vague text message with typos, you feel a rush of happiness that a man who is obviously liked by so many other women is interested in you. When Boring Bobby sends you a grammatically correct text message that leaves you in no doubt that he likes you, you feel little emotion, but if you want to create a family, and I do believe this is the best outcome for you, I advise you to ignore the text message from Exciting Eric and respond to Boring Bobby. This is what it will take for you to avoid the fate of cat ownership and anti-depressant addiction that is becoming the norm for women whose distorted instincts push them into relationships with men who will never commit to them.

It's likely that you will interpret Boring Bobby's behavior as needy, but such a man will be there for you in the long run, unlike an exciting man who is displaying signals that he doesn't need you at all. Some women will find it impossible to accept that they should chase after Boring Bobby, but if you delay doing so until you're 35 or older, you'll find that the Boring Bobbies have disappeared and all that's left for you is to settle down with Weird Walter.

You experience emotional butterflies with Exciting Eric in part because you grew up in a society that tells women to behave like men and have careers. I know this because I have been to countries such as Ukraine, Russia, and Serbia where women do not have successful careers and Boring Borises clean up with the best women. My exciting clown game in Ukraine produced pitiful responses because there is practically no advantage for girls there to have a short-term fling with a man they can't imagine providing for them in the long term. Once I had toned down my clown game and become Boring Roosh, where I flaunted my stability instead of my adventurous side, I got more results in the form of mini relationships.

My experiences in more traditional countries tell me that the type of man a woman finds attractive depends more on her environment than on her genetics. If you are materially comfortable and have been programmed by feminism, you will gravitate towards Exciting Eric. If you're in a resource-poor environment and have not been programmed by feminism, you will gravitate towards Boring Bobby. When all of your survival needs are being met and the culture is feeding you toxic messages, the switch is flicked for you to go from being attracted to Boring Bobby to Exciting Eric. By consciously resisting attention from the Exciting Erics, you can focus on men who are more likely to provide and protect.

You may even have noticed the switch happening to you as you climbed the ladder of financial stability and material comfort. When you were on the lowest rung of the ladder, struggling to make ends meet, you probably sought out men who displayed more provider traits compared to when you earned a good income and didn't have to worry about necessities. Think back to the boys you were attracted to as a teenager and compare them to the past few men you've liked to see if this holds true for you.

Another problem with having a career is that, because of your strong need for material security, it is extremely difficult for you to accept dating a man who makes less money than you. The harder you worked on your career to earn a high income, the fewer men you'll find suitable for marriage. The same principle holds true for women who refuse to date men that are shorter than them. This isn't a problem if a woman is 5'3", but if she's 6'3", her pool of prospective men will be tiny. Women who desire Exciting Erics that *also* earn a high income (over six figures) are the most likely to fail at finding a husband.

Strangely enough, the poorer you are, the bigger the pool of men you'll find attractive. The easiest way to drastically hurt your chances of finding a husband is to earn a high income, because you'll subconsciously rule out any man who makes less than you, even if his income is healthy and his character outstanding.

Knowing why you're attracted to Exciting Eric won't immediately stop you from desiring him. This desire will only diminish slowly over time. I used to look for Sexy Stacy with her flirty behavior, revealing clothing, and "come hither" face, but now I seek out Bookworm Betty or Virgin Vicky, who is shy and slightly awkward with understated beauty.

Being attracted to the "librarian type" didn't happen to me overnight. It was a process that took years after repeated experiences with Sexy Stacys taught me they are not suitable for starting a family. The same will happen to you once you realize that the Exciting Erics of the world are good for fleeting excitement and cheap thrills but little more.

What Men Want

When a man meets a girl for the first time, he instinctively puts her in one of two boxes: orgasm or love. The cues that help a man to decide in which box to put you are based on your appearance, behavior, personality, and how he met you. He will put you in the orgasm box if you flaunt your sexuality, are flirtatious or exceedingly comfortable around men, like to consume alcohol or drugs, frequent venues or dating sites where women congregate for sex, or have a reputation that suggests you've been with a lot of men. This type of girl indirectly says: "I am comfortable with sex, I am good at it, and I will not make you wait long before you can access my vagina."

Even though an orgasm girl has a high notch count, she will try to conceal it by saying things such as, "I'm not that easy," "A man has to work for this," or "I'm not that type of girl." Does a virgin or a girl who's had few sexual partners have to say these things? No, she *lives* the lines through her behavior and does not have to make verbal statements to confirm it. Only a promiscuous woman uses manipulation in an attempt to bridge the gap between who she is and who she wants to be seen as.

A man places a girl in the love category if she displays shyness, gentleness, grace, meekness, reliability, honesty, elegance, or inexperience. A man assumes that it will take more time before such a girl sleeps with him. For this reason, some men have given up on her in frustration. Now just because a man knows you're not promiscuous doesn't mean he won't see you as a challenge and go for the pump and dump. He may even pretend to want a relationship with you in order to get sex, but almost all players will give up once it becomes clear you won't put out within a certain period of time, usually five dates. The love girl serves up a physical obstacle course that only a man who shares her values and wants to be her long-term partner can overcome, while the orgasm girl serves up a verbal obstacle course that a man with even basic game can beat.

The fact that many men will still try to pump and dump a love girl tells you everything you need to know about the modern man. Many men have only sex and money on their minds and are not capable of anything more. The orgasm girl will often succumb to these men because she's weak and finds sex both validating and pleasurable. The love girl, on the other hand, uses her willpower to reward the man who also has willpower. However, even if you do wait a long time before rewarding Boring Bobby with sex, it doesn't guarantee he won't lose interest—it only *reduces* the odds that he will. This is why in the past, women didn't have sex with a man before marrying him. Whenever you have sex before marriage, you're rolling the dice since a man is free to walk away afterwards.

Men usually find it humorous when women say, "It's so hard to understand men." Put a woman in front of us and we either want sex or love from her. Mostly it's sex, because this is all we may currently want out of life, or we think you're only attractive enough for sex alone. For every 100 men who are interested in you, I estimate that 60 would only want to have sex with you once, 30 would want a friends-with-benefits arrangement, seven would like to be in a monogamous relationship with you but not marry you, and only three would like to marry you. If you display signs of being a Sexy Stacy, an even greater proportion will only want sex, and practically none will be willing to commit to marriage.

If a man has been feeding his devil for a long time, and most men have, he's not going to want love from a girl who is capable of providing it. You may think a man is stupid for passing up on such a girl, but there are cultural forces at play that encourage a man to seek only sex, which means you will *not* be able to change a man's mind if he just wants sex, no matter how virginal and amazing you appear, and giving him sex with the idea that it will make him more attached to you will actually do the opposite, because it will feed his devilish desire to seek out even more fun with other women. The solution is to increase the likelihood of meeting a man who has *already decided* to feed his angel before he meets you and focus on identifying the three men out of 100 who are prepared to marry you.

I know it's frustrating that so many men just want to use you for sex, but from the standpoint of men surveying the available women in their local environment, it's the most logical default option to have. For every woman like you who has traditional leanings, there are thousands who don't. For every woman who would choose a Boring Bobby over an Exciting Eric, there are hundreds who wouldn't. For every woman who wants to wait for sex, dozens give it up to men they barely know. For every woman who aches to be a good wife, several would take advantage of the divorce laws to ruin their husbands.

In any society, men are a reflection of the women, since it's women who ultimately decide whether or not sex happens. When a society degrades and sex becomes no big deal, a cheap act of mutual masturbation rewarding exciting and sexy men, it becomes logical for a man to mimic asshole behavior and only go for sex. In such an environment, the good man looking for a wife is being rather illogical because his strategy is far more likely to fail. Good men will always disappear in cultures polluted with feminism, where women have casual sex for fun while pursuing careers above family.

Another feature of men worth understanding is that many of them go through two life stages. The first is the player stage. It coincides with the peak of a man's testosterone and can best be described as "I want to have fun." He wouldn't know a perfect wife if one knocked him upside the head because his hormones are raging and all he can think about is sex. His devil is firmly in control and he is more satisfied with sleeping around than with experiencing love with one girl. It doesn't matter how perfect you are or if you're an ideal girlfriend, because if a man is in this stage, he will be completely unable to recognize your true value. Unless you think a man has reached the end of his player stage, is tired of sowing his royal oats, and is listening more to his angel than his devil, you'll be disappointed by your efforts to get him to commit.

The second stage men go through is "I'm ready to settle down." His testosterone level has peaked, his life has become more stable, and he doesn't experience as much joy when sleeping with random girls. In this stage, if he meets a girl of value, he will make an effort to commit to her, but until he finds her, he may *still* seek out easy sex. Understand that the male sex drive is far more intense than yours. When a woman is horny, she still remains quite selective about the man she eventually sleeps with, but when a man is horny, he will sleep with just about anything. All men have stories of the "hogs" and "beasts" they have slept with who were way below their standards, and despite these negative memories, they are only one sexual emergency away from doing it again.

To be a man means you are possessed by the monster hanging between your legs. Only through conscious effort, prayer, and understanding of what the monster is doing to me can I begin to resist the kind of sex that doesn't lead to love. This is tough but possible for men in the settle-down stage, but it's impossible for men who are still in the player stage.

Beware that the stages don't always correlate with age! Logically, you'd think that a man between the ages of 18 and 25 will be in the player stage, and that he will ease into the settle-down stage as he gets older, but every man has his own unique clock. In fact, some men are in the settle-down stage when they are young, and then a heartbreak or two puts them into the player stage where they want to make up for lost time. The more traditional a man's upbringing, the more likely he will be in the settle-down stage at a younger age, but this probably won't be the case if he was raised in a big city where casual sex is the norm.

To find out what stage a man is in, simply postpone sex and see how he reacts. A man in the player stage will almost never wait more than five proper dates for sex, while a man who is ready to settle down can wait far longer. Completely ignore what a man says about the things he's looking for in a woman—most of it is manipulation. It's too easy to tell a woman what she wants to hear, usually by being vague and mysterious. If a guy says he's looking for a girlfriend but starts having a temper tantrum when you don't put out by the second date, you're dealing with someone in his player stage. I have long advised men that a girl's actions say more than her words. The same also applies to men.

If I met my dream girl during the fun stage of my life, I would date her longer than a promiscuous girl, but it would just be a matter of time before I started seeking more fun and novelty. If I meet my dream girl today, I would want to impregnate her immediately and take care of the resulting family, but until then, I would still entertain the option of sleeping around if it didn't require much effort. A lot of heartache for the typical woman comes from thinking that a man who wants to have sex with her can be eased into a relationship, but men can separate the two without difficulty. Women are doing the same, putting out quickly for sexy men they meet on Tinder, often within minutes of meeting face-to-face, but playing harder to get with other men. For a long time, women were able to hide their true nature, but men are becoming wise to the warning signs and red flags, thanks in part to men like me who create internet platforms to share knowledge about women.

Within three minutes of meeting a girl, I can estimate her notch count, her attraction buttons, and her long-term potential. Even her profile picture on social networking gives me valuable information. Since I'm ready to settle down, I can't risk choosing a potential wife who is promiscuous. Men who are interested in creating a family will also train themselves to identify warning signs of promiscuity so they don't risk marrying someone who may cheat on them. There are so many horror stories online about divorce that a man who doesn't properly screen a potential wife will be in for a bumpy ride.

If a man chooses not to commit to you, it's because of two reasons. First, he's in his fun stage thanks to his horniness, or the culture is so broken that rationally it's the most suitable stage for him to remain in. Secondly, he could be in his settle-down stage but doesn't see you as his dream girl. In the latter case, he will choose not to commit to you because he thinks you have a history of promiscuous sex, he doesn't trust you, he doesn't feel an intimate connection with you, he doesn't think you'd make a good wife or mother, he sees you as being too negative, you don't meet his beauty standards, or a number of other reasons he may not even be conscious of. You won't be able to be every man's perfect girl, but there are things about yourself you can change to appeal to men who are settling down in a way that is healthy for you and makes you feel better about yourself.

The Dream Girl

There is an old saying that goes, "For every old shoe there is a foot." No matter how weird, strange, or unique you are, there is someone somewhere in the world who is right for you and who will love you completely for the person you are. Don't make any changes to your beliefs or appearance and simply wait for that one man to appear and sweep you off your feet as if you were living in a Disney cartoon. I say this only half-jokingly, because I truly believe that every person will eventually encounter someone who accepts them totally and is prepared to dedicate their life to them. There's only one problem: you may not like that person.

The drawback with morphing into the type of person you *think* the opposite sex likes is that you lose yourself in the process. I believe I am an introvert by nature, but I forced myself to display extraversion to attract girls, and felt like I had to keep on being extraverted so that the girls I attracted wouldn't lose interest. In other words, I became an actor. Before every date, I had to raise my energy level and prepare myself to be the most interesting man in the world. I could keep this charade going for only a few dates. Since then, I've learned to make only external changes that don't conflict with my character and that I don't mind making, whether or not girls are in the picture.

To maintain my physical attractiveness, I go to the gym about six times a month, groom my beard, and trim my body hair. I do these things even if I'm not on the dating market, so they don't conflict with my character and create inner conflict. To allow women to connect with me, I put myself out there by approaching women I like, and I can provide a 30-minute burst of lively conversation. Then I relax and see if the girl invests in the interaction. Staying attractive, approaching women, and being social is definitely work, but they don't make me feel that I'm not being true to myself. If I do all these things and still don't meet a girl, I will see whether there's some other minor thing I can change, but I won't do anything that makes me feel bad about who I am, and neither should you.

Before I give you advice on how to increase your chance of being seen as a man's dream girl, it's important to review the differences between the masculine and the feminine.

The masculine uses aggression, strength, and power to *take* from the world. A man hunts for animals, he works hard for money, and he pursues women. If a man walks out his front door and takes a long walk, nothing will happen to him—no one will present him with an opportunity and no woman will approach him. Nothing ever happens unless he makes it happen.

The feminine uses beauty and vulnerability to *receive* from the world. She is a worm on a fishhook that attracts the masculine who wants to conquer her, take her, protect her, and keep her as his own. If you walk out your front door and take a long walk, something may happen. A man, or several men, may try to start conversations with you, especially if you dress in an appealing manner. Your goal should be to maximize your femininity to the point where the masculine wants to come into your world and take you. Use your beauty and feminine grace as the bait for a big fish to come and take a bite.

Once a man optimizes his value, the best way for him to meet a girl is through constant action. Once a woman optimizes her value, particularly her beauty, the best way for her to meet a man is through *inaction*, by allowing the masculine to come into the feminine. The good news is that initially you have to take almost no risk beyond going outside, where men can evaluate your bait. Embracing the passivity of the feminine will ensure that men will pursue you through masculine action, which is why you should not make it easy for them by doing the work. The more effort a man has to make when he pursues you, the more he feels invested in you, and the more he feels that you are his girl.

You already have something that every single heterosexual man loves: a vagina. He is ready to jump through flaming hoops to get it, but the bad news is that every other woman also has one. Assuming a vagina is functioning and lubricating properly, penetrating one is so intensely pleasurable for a man that he is just about guaranteed an orgasm from even boring sex, whereas for you an orgasm is far from assured. Sleeping with a woman is like playing the slot machine in a casino and hitting the jackpot every single time, which is why a man will lie or scheme his way into one 10-minute instance of drunken sex.

Without having done anything, you already have a big chunk of juicy bait on your hook that gets men knocking on your door, but as you know, having a vagina is not enough to get the man you want. You have to ensure that your vagina is not the best thing about you, because if it is, you won't be able to retain the commitment of a man. Men will use you for sex until they get bored with your body and move on since there are many other vaginas of different colors, sizes, and textures to try.

The biggest complaint I receive from men is that modern women don't have anything to offer apart from their vaginas. In the past, a woman would be trained by her mother on how to please and serve men, or even attend finishing school, but today she is educated only so that she can have a career and make money, which doesn't enhance her bait. Sadly, most women have no idea how to please a man beyond sex, so their vagina is the main course of the meal they serve to a man instead of being the dessert. A man who meets you will initially see you in terms of your vagina, but every minute he spends with you should prove to him that you offer so much more value beyond it.

My task is to stack your hook with enough bait that a man would have to be an idiot to see you in sexual terms only. This definitely won't be easy in our sex-obsessed world, but my hope is that the advice I give is compatible with your character, just like how going to the gym regularly and carefully grooming my thick, lush beard fits nicely with mine while making me more attractive to women. Understand that even if your hook is stacked with the best bait in the world, a man in his fun stage won't be able to recognize your value, so our strategy is intended only for men who have already made the conscious decision to settle down, which you need to confirm before you have sex with him.

Before you attempt to stack your hook, you have to know the five things that a man wants from a woman. They are part of a hierarchy: once a woman satisfies a man's first need, he will seek to satisfy the need above it, and so on. The first need, unsurprisingly, is sex—or the upcoming prospect of sex—with a physically attractive woman. If you do not meet this need, it matters little what other bait is on your hook. A man must see you as pretty or beautiful and have a strong desire to have sex with you, and this desire must be completely sated as the relationship deepens into marriage, or he may be motivated to seek out another woman.

Going back to our shoe analogy, there will almost always be a man who is sexually attracted to even the ugliest of women. The problem for a woman isn't so much the lack of men who want to have sex with her but gaining the interest of a good man who will stick around afterwards. If you're not that beautiful, you will have to be more realistic with your standards. Otherwise, you'll keep on getting pumped and dumped by men you wish would stick around but won't because you don't have enough bait to offer them for the long term.

It's not fair that a woman's beauty, or lack thereof, puts a ceiling on the type of man she can get, just like how it's not fair for short men that height is one of the biggest qualities that women desire, but the good news is that there is a lot you can do to improve your appearance. Men also have options: they can become rich and famous to attract beautiful women. This doesn't necessarily lead to "true love," but since a man's most immediate need is sex with an attractive woman, it is usually sufficient to provide him with some happiness. I'll provide more details later on how you can improve your appearance because it's the most important piece of bait you can put on your hook.

I know you don't want to hear how important looks are, because for years the culture has lied to you that it's "only what's on the inside that matters," but denying the hard truth won't improve your situation. The reality is that beauty is *initially* the most important need for men, and it determines how much they will invest in you. You have to work with this fact of male nature instead of fighting it.

A man's second need is centered on intimacy, friendship, and companionship. Simply put, a man wants a woman he can spend time with in a way that reduces his stress. You're doing the opposite if you are demanding, flakey, unreliable, moody, or challenging. As I mentioned earlier, a woman often projects her attraction buttons onto a man, so because she may respond well to a man who treats her badly, she thinks that men also prefer to be treated that way, not understanding that the sexes have different natures. More commonly, an unhappy woman will take out her frustrations on the nearest available target—her man.

The only time a man will put up with negative behavior that increases his level of stress is when he's aching to satisfy an urgent need for sex. I will tolerate a certain level of flakey and princess behavior if I'm trying to extract sex from a girl, but once my desire has been sated, the tolerance ends. A woman can get away with grotesque behavior if the man she's with is crippled by his need for sex. Some men are so weak that they can be enslaved by a woman through sex alone, but unless you want a mindless sex slave, you'll have to be a pleasant person who makes a man feel at ease, comfortable, and relaxed.

A man's third need is a woman who makes his life easier or better. The best way you can meet this need is by doing household chores or other tasks so that your man can pursue his work or hobbies. My last girlfriend helped me by doing my laundry, making my morning coffee, and cooking meals, which allowed me to finish my work earlier and spend more time with her in the evening. Since women demand so much of a man's time, if my girlfriend or wife doesn't take care of some of my chores or tasks, the relationship will put me in a hurried state and increase my tension. The simplest way to help your man is to dedicate at least 10% of the time you spend together towards cleaning for him, preparing meals, or doing other chores.

One problem the average man has is that his woman wants to monopolize all of his free time. She expects him to entertain her endlessly as if he were a smartphone with a penis. Be *less* of a time sink by creating the illusion that having you in his life saves him time. If we spend six hours together and you spend one of those hours cooking, cleaning, or shopping for me, you will take a load off my back and decrease my stress. If you also satisfy my need for sex, I'm well on my way to seeing you as a dream girl who is worth a serious commitment.

Ignore the feminist complaint that cooking and cleaning for a man is filling the role left absent by his mother, particularly when you consider that a man's role of providing and protecting, which women innately crave, is what your father did (or what you wanted him to do). There is a definite overlap between a mother and wife and a father and husband, and this has been a fact of nature for millennia, but the roles are not identical.

The girls I've had successful relationships with often remarked how I shared a handful of traits with their fathers. A woman who is happy with her father because he protected her will logically seek out a husband who has similar traits. A man who is happy with his mother because she was loving and nurturing will logically seek out a woman who also shares similar traits. Good mothers who fulfill their natural role will appear the same, just as good fathers will. Unless you had a bad father, it is certain that a good man will have some of his attributes.

A man's fourth need is centered on loyalty, honesty, and faithfulness. When a man finds out that his woman lied or deceived him, he loses trust in her, and unless that trust is regained, the relationship will die. This is especially true if the lie involves another man. Female infidelity is a man's most serious concern because it can result in another man impregnating his woman and him being cucked into raising a child who is not his. On the other hand, if a man cheats, the worst that can happen is that he will have to pay child support to a mistress, a painful outcome for sure, but one that is far less catastrophic than raising a child you mistakenly thought was yours.

Men tend to be jealous because it reduces the likelihood that they will be cuckolded. There's a fine line between imposing standards on your wife so that she doesn't put herself in a position where cheating could occur and obsessing about where she is every second of the day, but I advise men to be firm in not allowing women to "meet" a man who is "only a friend." Many men use platonic friendship as a strategy to get laid. They orbit a woman under the guise of friendship and strike when they sense an opportunity. Unless the orbiter is obviously a sodomite, I do not permit my woman to have one-on-one encounters with other men.

If a couple is serious about their relationship, they should avoid being alone with someone of the opposite sex, especially at venues where alcohol is served, but even coffee meetings should be avoided. The problem with permitting an "innocent" daytime coffee date, for example, is that a woman may break the spirit of her commitment by scheduling it at a time that pushes the date into the evening, or by meeting a man she suspects has a romantic interest in her. Whatever rules you and your man decide on, understand that he may spend an inordinate amount of time testing your faithfulness, and if he doesn't, it's because he's hopelessly naïve or you're a good woman who is not giving him any cause to worry.

Honesty is also essential when it comes to telling your man how many sexual partners you've had. If you tell a man that you've been with, say, five men in your life, and he later finds out there were other men you didn't mention, it is fair grounds for him to dump you, because such a lie erodes trust in the relationship and causes him to question the other things you've said or done.

I advise you to *never lie,* because even if you get away with a lie today, you will be found out tomorrow, which will put your relationship—and the huge amount of time and effort you've invested in it—at risk. When I'm only trying to get laid with a promiscuous girl, I may lie about my age or backstory to help me have sex quickly, but when I'm with a girl I can see myself staying with, I am sure to tell the truth, even if it makes me look bad. Otherwise, the relationship will be severely damaged once she discovers my lie.

What you will be tempted to do, and which I sometimes do, is lie by omission. When I first meet a girl, I do not tell her that I'm the writer of more than a dozen X-rated sex guides. Experience has taught me that a girl will have trouble accepting this until she has developed strong feelings for me. So without lying, I simply leave it out and vaguely state that I have an "internet business." When she later finds out about my books, I explain the details to her and hope for the best. I'm still lying because I omit damaging information, but it gives me plausible deniability that I didn't "technically" lie. Not only is this shady, but there's no guarantee it will work, and there have been times for me when it hasn't.

We naturally want to hide negative things about ourselves so that we appear to be the ideal partner, because we've all made serious mistakes in the past, not to mention the flaws in our character that we want to downplay, but outright lying will almost always come back to haunt you, while lying by omission creates an atmosphere of distrust. It's better to deal with the repercussions of an unfavorable revelation now, when the stakes are low, than when they are higher and life-altering.

A man's fifth and final need is to be accepted as he is. We want a woman who swallows whole both our strengths and our flaws without attempting to change us into someone else. The problem is that as soon as you get involved with a man, you start to work at elevating his status by pushing him to improve his appearance or make more money. Although it's understandable that you want your man to be the best that he can be, he will resent you for it unless he specifically asked you for help.

It's even worse when you try to change his habits for your benefit alone. I once had a girlfriend who criticized me for wanting to read the news during breakfast instead of entertaining her. Another girlfriend complained that I left hair on my bar of soap that she didn't even use. More diabolical is when a woman tries to reduce the time a man spends with his friends or family to make him more dependent on her. If a man has an irritating habit or routine that wasn't an obstacle to entering a committed relationship with you in the first place, your best course of action is to take a deep breath and let it go, because I guarantee that you have habits that he wouldn't mind changing as well. Ask a man how successful his mother was at changing his habits and you will quickly learn that nagging simply breeds conflict.

Accept your man for who he is. I feel a profound bond with a woman who understands me and my work because I know how hard it is for two individuals to truly understand one another. If I do something stupid or silly, and my woman smiles or lovingly gives me a rub, I will feel that I have found the perfect woman, because at the end of the day, a man wants a woman who allows him to be himself, warts and all. When a woman is constantly criticizing my behavior or calls me "weird" in a condescending manner, I start to feel self-conscious and reach for the actor's mask to hide who I really am so that I won't be judged, but once I put on that mask, the connection is broken.

I apply this advice to myself when my woman does something I don't like but which doesn't hurt me. I take a deep breath and accept that she is her own person who also wants to be accepted as she is and not be forced to wear an actress's mask. Of course, there are standards when it comes to our partner's behavior and appearance, but the relationship is not benefited when you try to change the little things that are not causing real harm.

What do you think will happen if you satisfy all five needs? If a man considers you attractive, you give him sex (or an implied promise of future sex), he enjoys spending time with you, you improve the quality of his life, you prove yourself to be honest, you accept him for who he is, *and* he's in the settle-down stage of his life, he will be more than eager to start a family with you. The problem is that most women today satisfy *only* the sex need of men who are in the fun stage of their life or they insist on pursuing sexy men whose value far exceeds theirs, leading to dead-end relationships that don't even last a month.

For the longest relationship you've had with a man, I guarantee that you fulfilled at least two of his five needs, possibly three. The more needs you fulfill, the longer the relationship will last, but it will end if you don't fulfill all five needs and the man is not ready for a commitment.

My most recent relationship failed because the girl was not honest. Since that one critical need was missing, I ended it. If a man ends a relationship with you, it's because you did not fulfill at least one of the five needs. Most men are not as analytical as me and operate almost entirely on instinct—they don't even know what their specific needs are. This means they may not be able to tell you exactly why they chose to walk away, but their subconscious told them that a need was not being fulfilled.

You might be thinking that fulfilling all five needs is hard work, and you're wondering what you get in exchange. To be with a man is to complement your feminine energy with the masculine. You are protected and provided for in a relationship based on love that creates a family. If you choose the right man, you will satisfy your need for intimacy and companionship, but understand that a man is not your clown, dildo, punching bag, or therapist. He's someone who holds your hand as both of you go through life, bonded to one another, but nothing more. Ideally, you should be so overflowing with feminine energy and love that fulfilling these five needs brings you pleasure and contentment instead of seeing them as a burdensome sense of duty.

Men are as flawed as you are, but they are given tools by nature that allow you to live in balance and harmony with existence and God by experiencing love and creating life yourself. When you're in your twenties, at the peak of your beauty and with no shortage of male attention coming in from all directions, you imagine the party will continue forever, but once you reach your thirties, you discover that the music does indeed stop, often abruptly, and unless you secure the commitment of a man who loves you, there won't be much to look forward to apart from a shallow materialistic existence.

It's not your fault that you don't automatically under-stand the needs of men, because you've been pushed into doing everything but understanding them. How many hours have you spent in university attending classes, doing homework, and taking exams? How many hours have you spent working in drab offices? How many hours have you spent consuming feminist-approved television shows, movies, magazines, blogs, and videos? And how many more hours have you spent on your smartphone uploading photos for validation or communicating with people you no longer care about? It all adds up to tens of thousands of hours, a colossal amount of time.

What does it say about society that you're encouraged to waste all that time without ever learning how to connect with the opposite sex? What does it say about men who spend thousands of hours watching pornography or learning game to get laid instead of looking for love? Even if you're ready to love a man and be loved by him, most of the men you meet are so disconnected from the positive side of their masculine nature that they will remain locked in their fun stage, but remember that there is a foot for every shoe, and you only need to find one shoe to make it work.

Beauty Bait

Before you can get into a relationship with a man, you first have to attract him. Since men are very responsive to a woman's beauty, this will be relatively easy. I'm going to focus on two areas that will disproportionately maximize your beauty: the length of your hair and your weight. If you want most men to see you as beautiful and you want to widen your pool of potential mates, grow out your hair as long as reasonably possible and maintain a slim figure.

A man *must* be attracted to you physically before he will begin to attach himself emotionally, which is not necessarily true for you. If he's strongly attracted to you, he will be prepared to invest *a lot* of time and effort in order to have sex with you. During the mating dance, you'll have the opportunity to satisfy his four other needs and display your true value. If he recognizes that value and is no longer in his fun stage, there is a good chance that a committed relationship will develop. Most women are not genetically ugly, but they chop off their hair and become overweight, sharply reducing the number of men who are willing to get to know them for anything beyond sex.

Another benefit of maximizing your beauty, even to the point where it may intimidate some men, is that you weed out men who purposely approach less attractive girls solely because they see them as an "easy" score, something I have done countless times in nightclubs. You may actually be approached by *fewer* men as you become more attractive, but the men who do approach will have stronger attraction to you. I predict that if you improve yourself physically, you will go from attracting a large number of fun-stage men to attracting a smaller number of higher-quality settle-down men.

Having long hair and a slim body increase your attractiveness by denoting a superior level of health and fitness that can be passed on to potential offspring. If you've watched World War II documentaries that showed images of concentration camps, you'll have noticed that most of the prisoners lacked hair. This is because protein and other minerals are required to produce it. You will see the same in documentaries about starving African children. Instinctively, men associate less hair with bad health or infertility and more hair with good health and fertility.

Men may not even know that they noticed a woman because of her hair, but it's often the first thing they see. The more hair on your head, the more likely a man will have a favorable impression of you that activates his inner hunter. You know your hair is serving as beauty bait when both men and women compliment you about it soon after meeting you. This is the case with my elderly mother, who takes great pride in having long, thick hair.

Body size is also linked to fertility. Scientific studies suggest that a hip-to-waist ratio of 0.7, which is the typical hourglass figure, lends itself to higher fertility in women. It's no surprise that if men are shown pictures of women with various hip-to-waist ratios, they find the women with a ratio of 0.7 to be the most attractive. Obesity destroys the optimal ratio and elicits less attraction from men. While some fat on women is healthy, it will be unappealing to men once it alters your body shape into something resembling a soda can, which will appeal only to men who have a fat fetish and enjoy feeding their women to make them even fatter.

Fat feminists are hard at work trying to push the false notion of "beauty at every size," but they are laboring in vain because you cannot significantly change the tastes of a man who prefers his woman to not increase her risk of developing diabetes, gallstones, and heart disease. A man doesn't want to marry a woman who is shortening her lifespan due to a lack of self-control unless he is also doing so himself.

Slim girls with long hair wouldn't mind if the "beauty at every size" lie took hold, because it would reduce their competition. There are dozens of other tweaks you can make to your appearance, but if your hair is short and you're overweight, they won't significantly increase men's attraction for you and the effort they're willing to make to hunt you.

A tragic irony is that a woman will try to improve every area of her life *except* her hair and weight. She'll spend large amounts of money on clothing, double down on her career, pursue a master's degree, get breast implants, plump up her lips, wear designer eyeglasses that cost over $500, get a tattoo on her arm, inject Botox into her forehead, and pursue other enhancements that may end up giving her a plastic appearance. Apart from breast implants, very few men prefer the plastic look, and the ones who do are looking for fun and arm candy, not a wife. Beauty does not come with an expensive price tag or surgery—it comes with the "boring" effort of letting your hair grow and watching what you eat.

Any beauty advice I give you beyond your hair and your weight would be an attempt to tailor you to look like my personal dream girl, but based on my interactions with hundreds of men, most men prefer a look that leans towards natural and classic instead of overly done-up. I've never heard a man say "I wish she put on more makeup" or "I wish her lips were plumped up with fillers." You don't want to look like a street prostitute, but you have to show a hint of sexuality so that you will at least be noticed, which means not wearing baggy sweaters or pants that leave everything to the imagination.

One way to experiment is to adopt a certain look and observe the type of men who pay attention to you. If a particular outfit or makeup configuration results in you attracting the wrong type of guy, drop it from your repertoire. For example, I know that if I wear an expensive suit, I will attract older women who are inclined to relationships. If I go out in jeans and a snug V-neck that shows off my impressive muscles, I will attract younger girls who are more oriented towards fun. Since I prefer girls in the age range of 18 to 26, I tend to show more skin, but I know that this comes at the cost of meeting girls who want to use me for my body.

Let's discuss the specifics of how to have long hair and an ideal body weight. For long hair, simply do not cut it. I find that girls have a compulsion to cut their hair more often than necessary because of "split ends." Newsflash: men cannot tell if a girl has split ends! We don't even know what a split end really is.

Another excuse that girls use for cutting their hair is that it's "healthy." In my experience, women think that men perceive hair volume, health, and ends in the same way they do, but our primitive analysis of hair focuses almost entirely on its length and whether it smells good. If we look at your hair and think, "Wow that's long," you already have our attention, and we're busy evaluating your body and other features, even if your hair is ravaged by split ends.

Depending on your current hairstyle, you may have to go through an awkward phase that lasts several months before it starts looking good. Keep away from the scissors, use gentle hair products, and let it grow. Get it out of your mind that your split ends are making your hair look bad, and ignore other women who urge you to cut your hair in a spiteful attempt to sabotage your beauty. Grow out your hair until it's well past your shoulders before considering a minor cut to fix the ends. Then allow it to grow further until it reaches the middle of your back. If you're finding that your hair is growing slowly, consider increasing your protein intake and supplementing with biotin, which promotes hair and nail growth. Even women who are follically challenged can grow their hair past their shoulders.

I don't buy the excuse that long hair is "too hot" or "hard to take care of." Attracting top-shelf men does require some sacrifice on your part, and if you consider how much time and effort you've already invested in your education and career, making a fraction of that sacrifice to enhance your appearance is a small price to pay once you consider the benefits you will receive.

Achieving your ideal body weight is a bigger challenge and involves a more serious commitment. Your first aim is to achieve a weight that makes you look thin. This means no excess belly fat or fat on your thighs or rear that is starting to stretch your skin and develop cellulite.

There are two reasons many women fail to achieve their ideal weight. First, they think it all comes down to exercise. While exercise does burn calories, it also increases your appetite, which makes it harder for you to control your food intake. If you visit countries where many of the women are thin, you'll discover that they don't work out. Exercise doesn't have to be part of a weight-loss plan, although it will boost your health in general and combat the harmful effects of a sedentary lifestyle.

The second mistake women make is eating small meals throughout the day as if they were grazing cows. I challenge you to find a study proving that this is an effective way to lose weight (I'll save you the time: there isn't one). Constant eating keeps your insulin levels elevated with the result that your body is continually primed for converting food to fat without burning any of it. The solution is intermittent fasting. In simple terms, it involves skipping breakfast, eating only full-sized meals, and not snacking. Its effectiveness has been proved in the bodybuilding community.

Intermittent fasting is where you have a daily six-to-eight-hour window in which to eat. This keeps your insulin levels low and forces your body to burn fat. You are not allowed to consume *any* calories outside of the window period, meaning that you don't eat for 16 to 18 continuous hours a day, though you can drink water and tea or coffee without sugar or milk. When your stomach hasn't had any food for 16 hours, it shrinks and cannot handle a huge meal, with the result that you feel full faster when you do eat, naturally limiting your portion sizes. A suggested schedule is to eat lunch at 12pm, skip all snacks, and eat a second meal between 6pm and 8pm. The fact that you will be hungry before your first meal of the day confirms that you're burning fat without having to exercise, as suggested by the saying, "Hunger is fat leaving the body."

If you graze throughout the day and never feel intense hunger, it's unlikely you're burning any fat. This has the effect of keeping your weight high. You then go to the gym, thinking that a workout will accelerate weight loss, but it only increases your appetite, and you end up eating more. Working out doesn't even burn that many calories. Running a mile burns only 100 calories, which is less than a small chocolate-chip cookie. Unfortunately, some women have started to lift heavy weights to build muscles like a man, but bodybuilding only makes you look attractive to lesbians and bisexual men.

If you want to lose at least five pounds, I advise the following: eat two meals a day in an eight-hour window, do not snack at all, and abstain from all sugary drinks and "sport" waters (a teaspoon of sugar in coffee or tea is fine, but only during your eating window). All sodas, even those that contain artificial sweeteners, must be banished from your diet. For the first week you try this, you will feel ravenously hungry before your first meal of the day, but your body will quickly adapt. Do not worry about what you eat. Simply eat what will satisfy you without making you feel bloated or overly full. If you want dessert, eat it immediately after a meal, not as a snack hours later.

After one month, weigh yourself and see whether you've lost any weight. This will enable you to know what a baseline intermittent fasting program can do for you. If you didn't lose much weight, there are three variables you can adjust. First, reduce the window period from eight hours to six or less, resulting in you going hungry for longer, which will burn more fat. Second, reduce your portion sizes. Third, eat only one meal a day with perhaps a banana substituting for the second meal. When I lived in Ukraine, a country where most women are thin, I learned that many of them eat only one meal a day. I thought their thinness was due to genes, but it's entirely the result of effort.

Once you've adjusted one of the variables, wait a month before weighing yourself again. Has your weight gone down? If not, you'll have to tinker further. If you lost weight and are satisfied with how fast the pounds are coming off, stick to your eating pattern. Once you hit your ideal weight, you can relax your fasting program, provided you can maintain your weight month after month.

To maintain my weight of 185 pounds at a height of 6'2", I eat two meals a day that are spaced eight hours apart. I abstain from all snacks and sugary drinks. What I love about this eating schedule is that I don't need to be neurotic about what I eat. A meal is a meal, and I will eat whatever is put in front of me until I'm full, because I know that I can maintain my weight by sticking to my eating schedule alone.

Another bonus of intermittent fasting is that you don't have to go to the gym, which ironically may cause you to *gain* weight while making you appear bulky and masculine. A better solution when it comes to exercise, and one that is more enjoyable, is to install a pedometer app on your smartphone, head to a beautiful park, and do a few thousand steps while listening to the birds or your favorite music.

One of the reasons we overeat is because it gives us pleasure in a life that is void of deeper meaning. We are stressed out from work, lonely from a lack of loving relationships, and atomized in a little apartment with unlimited digital entertainment. We look for escapes like casual sex, alcohol, drugs, and food to make us feel good in the moment. When you break into a tub of ice cream, you feel happy because it's delicious, but when the pleasure stops, the weight gain begins and the unhappiness returns.

Look for pleasure in healthier relationships with men instead of from food or other substances. The irony of overeating is that the more you eat for pleasure, the fatter you get and the harder it is to experience love with a man, since most men are not attracted to overweight women. Once you achieve your ideal weight and wow-length hair, you're on your way to maximizing the amount of positive attention you get from men. It's now time to focus on how to create a good first impression when meeting men so that they will invest in you.

Lady Bait

Men place so much value in beauty that you don't need to have a perfect personality to retain the affections of your ideal man. This is not the case when teaching a man how to be attractive to a woman, who wants looks, humor, intelligence, confidence, ambition, and adventurousness— all in one man. Teaching game to men is so complex that an army of gurus has stepped up to the task, but thankfully things are much easier for you. Merely being perceived as lady-like will be enough.

An attractive first impression, combined with your long hair and thin figure, will compel a man to want to wait for sex and stick around long after it instead of pumping and dumping you, or if you are saving your virginity for marriage, stick around until sex happens on your wedding day. This assumes that you're looking for men who are not in their fun stage, because I must emphasize that if a man is still in this stage, there is *no* advice in the world that will make him commit.

The first lesson of creating a good first impression is don't pretend to be a man. As I have already discussed, men are not naturally attracted to a masculine essence unless they are feminine themselves. Do not *try* to be confident, outgoing, outspoken, demanding, or argumenta-tive. Do not *try* to be a leader. If you are in touch with your feminine core, this advice will be easy to follow, because it requires conscious effort and decades of training for a woman to consistently exhibit masculine traits.

When I meet a woman and she shakes my hand firmly and looks into my eyes with an icy stare while standing rigidly erect, I know she is consciously trying to appear confident, and hopes that I will value her for it. If she were my co-worker in an office, perhaps I might, but I'm looking for the mother of my future children, not a business partner. Her confidence tells me that she has spent time deliberately learning how to be a man. While it's okay for you to be outgoing if you're naturally outgoing, drop all of the masculine behaviors you've learned or are trying to exhibit.

A masculine man values a meek woman who defers to his lead. Allow this type of man to hunt you. Let him put in effort at each stage of the interaction (meeting, conversing, touching, exchanging contact information, setting a date, kissing, sex), while you observe, enjoy, and receive. Only when you see a man you like start to struggle or falter should you come to his aid with a strategic question, glance, or compliment that encourages him, but it's not your job to exhibit confident or domineering traits to maintain his desire. You will always attract the opposite of the energy you put out, so a confident woman who is "in charge" is more likely to attract a weak man than a masculine one.

Remember that the feminine energy is made to receive. Things happen to you because you are the one who is hunted. My masculine energy is made to take. Things happen to me only if I make them happen, because I am the hunter. The universe may place a beautiful woman in my path, and she may even make eye contact with me, but I have to accept the risk of rejection and make the leap to speaking to her, or the opportunity will be lost forever. The more we behave in line with our sex-linked nature, the more we will be ready to experience what the universe offers us.

As a modern woman, you have lived in part with the masculine and have received some rewards from that, such as an education, career, material comfort, or physical satisfaction from casual sex, but all of these things have also led to pain, confusion, and anxiety due to having two opposing energies clashing within you. The answer is to free yourself from the masculine that you have learned from the culture. Simply let go of all masculine ambition. Relax. Let the world come to you. Stop trying to hunt, grab, take, and achieve. Broadcast your feminine essence to the world so that a masculine man already accomplished in hunting, grabbing, taking, and achieving comes to share his offerings with you, taking you to a place of love and family.

The second lesson of creating a good first impression is to let a man be a man. Understand that it's not easy for a man to initiate a conversation with you. He's taking a risk that may lead to public humiliation, so if he's the type of man you want to get to know, don't attack, insult, or test him for trivial reasons. Men in their fun stage will appreciate a verbal "challenge" from a drunk girl in a club, but a man in the settle-down stage does not want to marry a woman with a prickly, immature attitude. Instead, give encouragement by keeping your attention solely on him and asking thoughtful questions that allow him to present the best of his character—his experiences, stories, ideas, opinions, intelligence, humor, and confidence. Judge him based on his innermost values instead of how he responds to an insult or trick, which he will interpret as a sign that you are stuck in your fun stage.

Interactions between men and women have degraded to such an extent that they now resemble a rap battle of tit-for-tat challenges, but this simply has the result of weeding out good men who want a lady instead of a hip-hop performer. It's better to adopt the pleasant attitude of "Okay guy, I will give you some time to show me who you are." Give him just enough encouragement so that he makes his presentation, but be careful about doing the work that he alone should do, because men only value women they have to work for. If you make it too easy for him by doing most of the talking or asking all of the questions, or even worse, by escalating the interaction, how can he possibly value you?

Women often ask me how they can get a man to ask them out. Apart from maximizing their beauty and remaining in the feminine, ready to receive, the answer is nothing! It's the man's job to take the risk of rejection, not yours. You are an antelope frolicking on the savannah, full of elegance, grace, and vulnerability. It's up to the strong lion to run after you. If you chase after the lion instead, he may think you are diseased in some way, driven mad by a parasite. He'll run away from you, no matter how hungry he may be.

If a man doesn't have the strength to initiate a conversation with you and ask you out, how likely is it that he will be able to provide for you and protect you in a relationship? How is he going to deal with hard economic times or tough situations that may threaten your survival? Unfortunately, modern men have been so thoroughly neutered by feminism that they have been made to feel like criminal harassers if they ask a woman out on a date, and therefore they may have the courage to do so only if they are under the influence of alcohol. At the other end of the spectrum, you find men who are completely fearless because they've turned seduction into a gimmick after having interacted with thousands of women for the main goal of getting sex. I expect that you will experience much frustration from meeting men who lack balance with how they try to seduce women.

Since results will not come quickly, you will be tempted to be more ambitious in your quest to find a man and adopt the masculine approach of trying harder, but this will fail because once you've maximized your beauty, the universe will put the ideal masculine man before you only when it's ready, not when you're ready. I estimate that your ideal match will be presented to you only once a year. No matter how big the city you live in, or how many men you manage to meet every month, you will be able to love only one or *maybe* two men of all the ones you meet in a year.

This fact also applies to men. Whether I meet five girls in a year or 5,000, I will not meet more than one who is worth a relationship. You cannot cheat or rush the universe. All you can do is to keep your eyes open and embrace the feminine. All I can do is to keep my eyes open and embrace the masculine. Remain beautiful and ready for the lion when he appears, at a time that will not be disclosed to you beforehand. Staying true to our natures, whether masculine or feminine, and being patient is the only formula for success when it comes to love.

The third and final lesson of creating a good first impression that will encourage a man to invest in you is to let him exhaust himself. Stand in his presence and watch as he does everything possible to attract you until he is visibly tired or runs out of things to say. When this happens, stare warmly into his eyes or ask him a question. Many women cut their interactions with men short, usually as a way to tease them, but this forces a man to take a *second* social risk to re-initiate contact before he has fully invested in you. Most men will not do this. While it's polite to say, "It was nice talking to you, but I want to get back to my friends," it should only be done with the expectation that a man will never return.

Allow a man to become mildly stressed about what he should do next to gain your favor. This does two things. First, it makes him invest in you. The more he's working, the more committed he will be to asking you out on a date and following through. Second, you get to see the other side of him. It's very easy for a man to put forward his best qualities while he's talking to you, but you also want to see whether he has negative traits that are likely to emerge only when he is frustrated, tired, or even angry. Stand still, receive his game, give warm eye contact, smile, let him run out of things to say, and observe how he recovers. If he fails to recover and chooses to give up, he's not ready to make an effort to get you, because if a man can't deal with the strain of keeping a conversation going, how will he overcome the bigger problems that arise during a relationship?

The most "discouraging" thing you will do is maintain eye contact but not talk much. For the first few dates, you should contribute about 30% to 40% to the conversation, which is not that discouraging in the grand scheme of discouragement. You should not cut him down or withdraw. You should not pay attention to other things in the environment or regularly break eye contact. If he's attracted to your beauty, and you allow him to be a man without acting like one yourself, he will jump through many hoops to maintain the interaction.

Personally, I don't like to work hard for an average girl I only want to have sex with, but if I'm highly attracted to a girl and sense that she has good values, not only will I work hard for her, but I will feel more satisfied if I do eventually get her because of the work I had to put in. My effort starts at the beginning when I first talk to her and continues when I try to date her and she insists on progressing very slowly towards intimacy. If she delays sex, I will stick around only if there is genuine attraction and I'm *not* in the middle of my fun stage.

It's worth discussing the differences in behavior between the promiscuous girl in her fun stage and the potential wife in her settle-down stage. The promiscuous girl does not want men to think she's a slut, while the potential wife has no fear of that because her behavior is in no way slutty. When the promiscuous girl is attracted to a man, she will put up token resistance to his advances with phrases such as "I'm not that kind of girl" or "I don't usually do this." This is not because she really is difficult, but because she needs to manipulate how she is seen. The future wife, on the other hand, puts up genuine resistance to block a man in his fun stage from becoming intimate with her, not because she needs to manipulate him, but because she really doesn't want the shallow sex that he's offering. The promiscuous girl desires fast sex and will give in easily, but the future wife has already made a firm decision of when it's appropriate to be intimate with a man that is independent of the situation or her emotions.

If you simply want to sleep with sexy men, I don't have any advice on how not to appear promiscuous, but if you want to gain the commitment of a good man, you'll have to think logically about when to kiss and have sex so that you can filter out men in their fun stage while ensuring that those in their settle-down stage stick around. You want to move slowly enough with settle-down men that they recognize your value, all without appearing asexual like a nun. This will be most relevant when it's time for kissing and sex instead of early stage steps like having conversations, giving out your phone number, and agreeing to dates, to which you do not have to put up any resistance.

If a man you like is putting in the work by approaching you, sustaining the conversation, asking for your number or a date, and sweating it out to win your favor, there is no need to play "hard to get," because you haven't yet reached the intimacy stage. Use long conversations, particularly on dates, to get to know him by finding out where he is in life, what his past relationships were like, and what he wants in the future before deciding on whether or not to become intimate. Most of this will not involve much work on your part, besides optimizing your beauty, embracing your feminine side, and allowing the man to be a man and prove himself to you.

I suspect that women want specific steps on how they should interact with guys, but such a formula is more useful for the hunter than the hunted. Since men are expected to keep women in a constant state of entertainment and attraction, it's a simple matter to give them tips on conversation, body language, teasing, and so on. This is unnecessary in your case because once a settle-down man has decided to hunt you, he is certainly attracted. For him to be convinced that there is long-term potential, he has to feel genuine compatibility, which you cannot fake, and he has to be certain that you are not promiscuous, which will be implied if you make him wait a long time before having sex. All that's left for you is to be a woman. Your actions should subconsciously convey, "I like being hunted by you. Keep going."

Much of your demeanor should simply come down to having basic manners, which most modern women lack. Maintain eye contact with him, smile at his attempts to make jokes, encourage him by complimenting the behaviors you like, refrain from obsessively looking at your phone, dress pretty, ask questions that keep him engaged, share life stories that help him understand the kind of woman you are, and give opinions that aren't blatantly political or combative. This may sound like common sense, but you'd be surprised how many dates I've been on where women did the exact opposite.

Even if you do everything right, there is no guarantee that an interaction or date will produce the result you want. The dating game is brutal and requires a lot of failures before it yields success. Use each failure as a learning experience for dealing with the next man who wants to hunt you. I'm confident that rigorously screening out men in their fun stage will help to reduce the number of failures, but dating is not an app where you tap a button and an expected outcome occurs. Because it can take many years to find the right partner, I find it deeply upsetting that the culture tells women to delay finding a husband until they are in their late twenties or beyond.

In the end, the best you can do is embrace your passive feminine energy and allow a man to do most of the work. A warm glance will do more than trying to make him laugh with a sarcastic wisecrack. Giving him your undivided attention will do more than trying to appear intelligent. Letting him share his opinions will do more than getting into a political debate. All the while, you're allowing him to tire himself out and worry about how he can maintain the interaction. When you're in the presence of a potentially good prospect, focus on relaxing and receiving. If the man is right for you, he'll do almost everything else.

Meeting The Good Man

While there is some good in every man, for our purposes a good man is one who is ready to settle down and protect and provide for his woman. His attraction to you is oriented towards love and family, not the possibility of having casual sex.

Thirty or more years ago, the average man had little knowledge of how to relate to women, but today, thanks to being exposed to "red pill" content on the internet, he is more familiar with game, female behavior, marriage laws, and feminism. Much of this knowledge is aimed at maximizing his sexual success and minimizing failure in long-term relationships. There are still many naïve men out there, but it's becoming more difficult for women to fool men through deceit, lying, or manipulation, which is why we won't even attempt such trickery. Assume that the next man you like is wise to the ways of women, even if his outward behavior doesn't seem to indicate that he is.

If a man is ready for a relationship, he won't be seeking sexual excitement or adventure, so his game will be rusty.

This means it's unlikely you'll instantly feel butterflies or raw attraction. He will come across as stable, easy-going, logical, predictable, and shy. The accomplished player often displays the opposite traits. In fact, if you feel that a man is exciting and your emotional core feels an attraction that you can't explain, your devil may be pushing you into an interaction with a man who won't commit to you.

The good man will not know how to harness your powerful emotions to get sex quickly like the bad-boy player. He will be less aware of your emotional games. He won't be as pushy or aggressive and may require a lot of prodding to respond emotionally. While you will be focused on how you feel in the moment, he will look towards the future to ensure that the relationship will be stable and comfortable.

Even if most of your behavior towards him is based on becoming a nurturing and loving wife and mother, you will test him subconsciously when you are anxious about the relationship to find out whether he really is a strong man who can protect and provide. If he fails these tests, your devil will prompt you to window shop for other men. For example, no woman will admit that she desperately wants her man to say no to her, but this is exactly what a man needs to do from time to time to prove that he is at least strong enough to stand up to a woman. If a man folds easily to his woman, how will he protect her from an external threat that could harm the family?

I teach my male readers about the tests that women give and how it's essential to ignore women's emotional outbursts and say no when necessary, but this is not something you can simply read once on a website and master. If you follow my advice about reducing your anxiety, you will be disinclined to test men unnecessarily, making it less likely that you'll jeopardize the tranquility of your relationship.

It's unreasonable to expect you to be able to quickly identify a man's true intentions when it's cloaked behind his desire to have sex with you, because even the man who is ready to settle down may still consider having casual sexual encounters. Your strategy must be to postpone physical intimacy to weed out men who only want sex. I therefore advise you to kiss a man on the lips no sooner than date <u>two</u> and to have sex with him no sooner than date <u>nine</u>. (Oral or anal sex counts as sex.) This "two-ninths" policy serves the dual purpose of weeding out men who are in their fun stage and selecting for men who have a genuine connection with you. You are free to make him wait even longer.

Many a man will have a panic attack if you delay intimacy. He will become visibly frustrated and argue emotionally that you should kiss or have sex sooner. His frustration stems from being used to having sex quite fast, a possible sign that he's in his fun stage. Assuming he toughs it out to date nine or later, you'll have gathered a huge amount of information about him to make the right decision about having sex. If you do have sex by this time, it will just about automatically put you in a relationship with him.

A good man *will* wait until date nine to have sex with you. That is a trivial amount of time in the grand scheme of things when it comes to creating a loving bond with a potential wife. A player, or a man who sees you only as a sex partner, *will not* wait nine dates for a woman with whom he doesn't want a relationship. It will be far easier for him to find another girl.

You may be thinking, "What if a player decides to wait for nine dates just to pump and dump me?" This is possible but unlikely, because even diehard players will feel *some* guilt about spending that much time with you only to leave. This phenomenon is common among foreign men when they date Ukrainian girls, who wait for as many as five dates before having sex. On several occasions, I have ejected from a girl I was only sexually attracted to because I knew it would take too long to sleep with her. It doesn't make any sense to enter a relationship with a girl simply to bang her a few times. I'm sure these girls were disappointed that I didn't want a relationship with them, but what is more important is that they avoided getting pumped and dumped, which would have polluted their sexual history and reduced their ability to bond with a good man who wants to marry them.

The two-ninths policy also enables you to nurture your attraction with a good man who may not know all the game tricks. Attraction to a bad boy is often instant, because he knows how to hit many of your attraction buttons quickly, but a good man doesn't have this ability. Attraction to him will be built up through the rapport you should feel within nine dates. If the man is long-term material, but the attraction is not there by date nine, it is better to eject without having sex with him. If the man is not long-term material, but the attraction is present, it would also be best to eject. The only situation that can lead to marriage is where the man is long-term material *and* you are attracted to him.

Attraction doesn't have to include explosive passion. That's certainly nice to have, but passion fades quickly, often within a few years. If your relationship is based mostly on passion or physical attraction, it won't last. Shared values, comfort, a feeling of partnership, and attraction based on masculine-feminine polarity are far more likely to endure than passion or butterflies in your stomach. It's great if you can have it all, but it's virtually impossible for one man to have all the qualities you crave. Passion and raw attraction are of secondary importance for establishing a stable family and a good home for your children.

Many of the pieces are now in place. You have a good understanding of the positive and negative sides of your nature and that of men. You understand the poison the culture has fed you and why you should reject it. You know why you are attracted to assholes and why acting on this attraction is not conducive to creating a family. You know how to maximize the likelihood that a masculine man who is ready to settle down will pursue you, and more importantly, you know how to weed out men who aren't serious by not kissing until date two and having sex until date nine. We're missing one important component: where to find men.

I have a feeling that finding men is the least of your problems because you already know many environments and venues where men congregate. Now that your hook is stacked with beauty bait, simply insert yourself into an environment where men are present and wait until they hunt you. The game becomes one of patience and choosiness. Over 90% of the men who will come to you will not be suitable, and it may take one or two years until the right one does eventually find you, no matter how beautiful you are.

The biggest problem you'll encounter is that men have become so neutered that most have lost their hunting skills. This is on top of them being scared of rejection because they've internalized it as an indication of their self-worth. To maintain a positive self-image, men will try to avoid rejection at any cost. This is why men drink copious amounts of alcohol at night—it gives them the courage to hunt while minimizing the pain of rejection.

You need to make allowances for the fact that men are neutered and scared of rejection while simultaneously not doing any of the hunting for them. Remember: a man, neutered or not, will not value a woman he does not have to hunt, so he must initiate boldly and escalate each step of the interaction. What you can do, however, is indicate to a man that you will not bite off his manhood if he decides to take a risk on you.

Let's imagine two scenarios. In the first, I'm a single man who is ready to settle down, but I have not been laid in three months and am getting pretty horny. I don't like nightclubs, so I focus on meeting women during the day. The first pretty girl I see is walking quickly through the park while wearing headphones. She has a stern face and her lips are pursed. My hunter sense is picking up on several obstacles, but I am nonetheless attracted to her. I approach her and ask her where the lake is, and though she looks at me, she doesn't stop walking. I feel burned that a woman didn't even care to acknowledge my existence. I tell myself not to approach another girl who has the same type of presentation.

In the second scenario, I walk through the same park and notice a pretty girl reading a book while sitting on a bench. She has a pleasant expression on her face and looks up often. She notices me and we briefly lock eyes. A warm feeling flows through my body. I take a deep breath, walk up to the bench, and ask her where the lake is. She puts down her book and gives a long response that makes it easy for me to continue. We enter a conversation during which she discreetly judges my worth by asking a handful of strategic questions while doing only 30% of the talking. Since I meet her standards, she gives me her number when I ask her for it, and we plan a date.

Most women in public do not put out an inviting demeanor as in the second scenario, and then wonder why men never talk to them. Realize that men are always observing women and processing the temperature of their body language, whether during the day, at night, or within their social gatherings. If these signals are negative, they do not hunt. Just as a child learns not to touch a hot stove, a man learns not to talk to women who have a closed demeanor or who present themselves in the same way as the women who rejected him in the past. You can be the most beautiful girl in the city, but if your manner is not inviting, men will pass you up due to the fear of rejection. This is why many very beautiful women are approached less than women who are more average looking—the beautiful woman almost always has a snobby, standoffish demeanor that scares men away.

There are three things I recommend to increase the chances that a man will attempt to hunt you: move slowly, make eye contact, and smile. Moving slowly is the first step. It makes you appear more inviting, friendly, and helpless as if you were a wounded animal that is easier to hunt. In our minds, a vulnerable woman will not attempt to make us feel like crap if she doesn't like us. Another benefit of moving slowly is that it gives men more time to evaluate your beauty and come up with a way to meet you. If you're flying by, a man won't have enough time to decide whether you're his type and devise an ice-breaker.

If you're out in public, walk slowly as if you're not in a hurry to be somewhere. If you're at an indoor venue or party, plant yourself where you'll be highly visible and allow men to digest your presence instead of rapidly moving from one spot to the next. Be the wounded animal that all hunters notice and think they have a chance of capturing.

Second, make eye contact with men who meet your physical standards, and maintain eye contact for at least three seconds so they know it wasn't accidental. If a girl is walking slowly and makes extended eye contact with me, my heart immediately starts beating faster, because she's saying that she wants me to attempt to hunt her. I then evaluate her beauty, and if it meets my standards, I will think of a way to start speaking to her. Only a small percentage of men will act if you make eye contact with them, but it is a key step in increasing the number of those who will try.

Third, to *really* encourage a man, top off your eye contact with a smile. This will send a red-hot signal that you are physically attracted to him. Beware! You're now approaching—but not yet crossing—the line of doing the work that a man should do. You do not want to give a man an absolute money-back guarantee that he won't be rejected, because if he doesn't have to take some risk, how can he become invested in you? Start with moving slowly and making eye contact, and if these don't produce the desired responses, add a smile, but nothing more than that. An alternative to a smile is maintaining eye contact indefinitely, as if you're having a staring contest. However, most men will interpret a staring contest as showing less interest than a smile.

Even if you smile, most men won't approach you, no matter how attractive you are, because they fear rejection and have been programmed with feminist conditioning which tells them that talking to a woman is a form of "harassment." You may find that it's mostly minority men (black, Latino, and Middle Eastern) who respond more readily to your inviting demeanor since their "macho" background is more resistant to cultural neutering than is the case with white and Asian men, particularly in large multicultural cities.

To maximize the number of men you meet in public, try going for walks in crowded parts of your city for three to eight hours a week when the weather is warm. Wear a cute outfit and go for a slow stroll through a safe area where men will be present, especially around lunchtime or when the workday is ending. Do *not* put on headphones, because this will discourage men from trying. Depending on where you live, you may be overwhelmed by men or none will try to talk to you.

I'll be the first to admit that meeting people in public is not the best way to find love. It's more suited for loners who don't have the energy to spend long periods with other people. You may also be disappointed by how many men are scared to approach you even if you give them encour-agement with eye contact and a smile. On the positive side, if you live in a large city, you can go outside at any time and start fielding offers from hunters without having to depend on other people to organize events or meetups.

Experiment with different venues and assess the responses you get. Perhaps men don't approach you in parks and coffee shops but do so regularly in bookstores and museums. Always keep your eye open for a niche location that is conducive to men chatting you up. For example, you may know of a coffee shop with a shared table where men are always working on their laptops. Make eye contact and see what happens. Or maybe on your way home from work there's a hotel lobby where you can buy a cup of tea and be surrounded by successful businessmen. You'll be surprised by how many little goldmines exist within only a mile or two from your home.

In my city, I came up with a little trick at the library. I couldn't approach girls inside the library, but I could stay there until closing time and leave at the exact moment a girl I liked was also leaving. I would then "spontaneously" encounter her as we both walked out of the library at the same time. For you, the main strategy is to know where the men you like are located and then find a way to encourage them to hunt you. Your safety is the number-one priority, so do not explore strange or isolated areas of your city, especially after dark, or neighborhoods that have a bad reputation.

Two more ways to be hunted by men are through a social circle or loosely-based community. A social circle is composed of a group of friends and acquaintances who spend time together while a community is a group of mostly acquaintances who share one or two interests. The problem with modern society is that we've become so atomized that we may have only one social circle that consists of fewer than ten individuals. If your lone social circle does not include a man with whom you can develop a connection, you'll be forced to try other means.

By far the largest benefit of a social circle is that it's the safest and most fruitful way to meet a man, but if you don't have a large social circle, perhaps because you've moved away from your birth city or have friends that already got married, it won't be easy to join another one since they usually form in high school or college. The best you can do is attach yourself to an established social circle so that you are in a position to be invited to events where men are present.

A problem you may have with your social circle is that it's probably composed mostly of women, who tend to keep the best men in the group to themselves. If you have a friend who is single, she is unconsciously competing with you for men. She may even sabotage your efforts by throwing shade on your growing hair or thinning body. Men are often appalled that female friendships are marked by backstabbing and jealousy, so be on guard when dealing with your girlfriends.

Most people now rely on communities that are organized through the internet. They come in the form of language clubs, speaking clubs such as Toastmasters, salsa dance schools, and professional clubs that focus on job networking. The bonds that tie together the members of a community are much weaker than those of a social circle, but the turnover is higher and you'll have the opportunity to meet more men. Another benefit of a community is that—unless it's a girl's book club—it will almost always have a high ratio of men to women.

To maximize the potential opportunities from your social connections, I recommend that you say yes whenever you're invited to an event. Look your best, encourage men with your demeanor and gaze, be friendly to the other guests, and exchange contact information with potential acquaintances who have large social circles. Aim to attend at least a few social functions a month where you can meet acquaintances and have a decent man or two approach you.

If you attend the functions of a particular group several times but are not approached by high-quality men, try other groups.

The second way to meet men is to join communities that are based on a shared interest. In my hometown of Washington, D.C., professional networking groups are quite popular. Dance schools are also common, helping to select for a man who has some rhythm. Most communities are organized through social networking sites, so it may be a simple matter of logging on to Facebook to find out what events are being hosted in your city. Choose one that is likely to attract the type of man you want, go alone if you have to, place yourself in a highly visible area of the venue, and wait for men to chat you up. Because anyone can attend these events, you'll have to deal with a lot more men who are duds, so stay sharp when evaluating them.

If you believe in God, I strongly recommend that you attend or join a church and view it as a long-term strategy that may involve doing volunteer work. It is likely that single men who belong to a church will possess many positive attributes, including being in their settle-down stage. Make a list of two to four churches in your area that are compatible with your beliefs, check out the Sunday service of each, and then pick the one that most appeals to your spiritual needs. Go every week and occasionally attend church social functions.

While it's nice to be approached by attractive prospects when you walk out your front door, understand that men who hunt women outside of church or social-circle settings are less likely to be seeking long-term relationships. Invest in at least one tightly-knit community instead of solely relying on being approached in public.

I do not recommend internet dating, because most online men are in their fun stage, looking for easy sex. Hot guys will contact you using copy-and-paste messages they've perfected through trial and error, making you think there is genuine interest when all they really want is to have sex with you as quickly as possible.

Internet dating will also demoralize you because you will invest a lot of time to meet men who will end up being quite different in person to how they presented themselves online. For every internet success story, there are dozens of horror stories, including sour interactions where insults are exchanged.

Another downside of online dating is that it will make you *think* you are getting solid leads, causing you to invest less in a social circle or community. Trying to match with men while in your pajamas at home, instead of doing the work to build genuine connections in real life, will make you lazy. Ultimately, internet dating is more for women in their fun stage who want casual thrills. You should rely on social circles, communities, and public encounters as your three best ways of meeting men.

What should you do if men aren't approaching you? No matter where you go in the world, single men will attempt to have sex with women as long as they are approachable, no matter how ugly they are. I have witnessed unattractive women who were crippled, bald, or even lacking limbs get approached by men. If you're not being approached at all, it means you're going to places that lack masculine men, such as gay clubs, or you're putting out a masculine vibe that tells men you will crush their genitals if they try to talk to you.

Look in the mirror. Observe your movements, gaze, and smile. Are they warm and inviting? Ask a male friend for his honest opinion. Embracing the feminine is embracing the vulnerable. Lose any rigid confidence or sternness in your body language. This doesn't mean you should slouch or look sad, but have the look of a woman who needs help. If you were genuinely lost in a city, how would you appear? Wide-eyed, slightly concerned, hopeful. This is the vibe that will maximize the number of hunters who seek you out.

It might be that you *are* being approached but are failing to notice it. To explain what I mean, realize that *zero* women try to talk to me during the course of my day. They don't hold the door open for me, make small talk about the weather, or otherwise give me aid. If a woman does chat me up, no matter how innocuously, I have to assume that she wants to sleep with me or is filming some kind of internet prank video.

Whenever a man talks to you, for whatever reason, he is in fact approaching you, because if you were a 1,000-pound woman, he almost certainly would not have initiated the interaction. In most cases, these interactions are indirect and nonchalant, but if your response is positive in the form of smiling, giving him your full attention, or moving slowly, he'll continue the conversation and reveal his hunter intent. Since you've been approached by men so often since hitting puberty, it's likely that you don't recognize them as approaches but as low-level background noise.

Approaches are either indirect or direct. An indirect approach is when a man asks you for directions, holds a door open for you and smiles, makes a comment about the weather, asks about a book you're reading, or casually inquires about something in order to gauge your receptiveness. A direct approach is when a man starts with a compliment or clearly shows personal interest that leaves no doubt that he wants to get to know you. Since most men approach indirectly, don't expect cartoonish "Me hunt Jane, me big man" behavior.

A more common problem is being approached by a man you don't feel attracted to. The reality is that both men and women want a romantic partner who has high value, often above their own. Only once it becomes clear that they can't get such a partner do they start to be more realistic about their standards. The good news for men is that their value naturally increases as they age into their thirties because women prize experience more than youth. The bad news for women is that their value goes down as they age into their thirties because men prize youth and beauty more than experience. Once you reach the age of 30, you should be lowering your standards each year, which is something that most women fail to do.

Even if you drastically increase your beauty, there will be a limit to the type of partner you can attract. For example, if I spend ten years improving my value but am upset that I still can't get my ideal girl, the problem is not women but *me* and my unrealistic standards. The logical response is to lower them while the emotional response is to say that all women suck and marriage doesn't work. Unfortunately, many women who fail to find love become bitter and say that men "act like boys" or "are afraid of strong women." Complaining can feel cathartic, and I've certainly done my share of it, but unless you adapt to your environment and check your standards against an honest appraisal of your worth, it will be impossible to succeed with relationships.

It's unlikely that you will gain the commitment of a man who is more attractive or has higher status than you, although such a man will definitely sleep with you for fun. A famous male celebrity will fornicate with a groupie, and be excited to do so, but this doesn't mean he will ask for her hand in marriage. A man's standard for sex can be so low that you may be able to sleep with millionaires, sports stars, and other famous men, but none of them will offer you anything more than a sugar daddy type of arrangement. This means that you should not confuse the sexual attention you've received from men—particularly when you were in your physical prime—with men who would be willing to commit to you.

Men have a term for a woman who has been pumped and dumped by a man whose status was so high that it has distorted her view of the type of man she thinks she can land in the future: alpha widow. She holds out for years, waiting for a man of equal or higher status to come along, but it never happens and she fails to marry, or she marries a man with the intention of cheating on him if her alpha stud returns one day. It's likely that you will not find another man whose status matches that of the highest-status man who gave you attention in the past, so don't base your standards on the top two or three men who have given you sexual attention.

Men are often mystified by the complexity and detail of a woman's shopping list for her ideal man. Most of the time, the man they are describing doesn't exist in real life. If your list has more than three or four qualities, chances are you will fail, and even four qualities may be too many. The older you get, the shorter that list will have to become, to the point where it contains only one or two qualities. This advice is too dreadful for some women, because they don't want to date lower than they've had in the past, but they must understand that their value in the eyes of men is lower than when they were younger, as unfair as that may be.

Many feminists are trying to brainwash men into finding older and fatter women more attractive, but until they succeed, and I promise you that they won't, you'll have to lower your standards as you age, sometimes substantially so. If one year after reading this book you're not satisfied with any of the men you've met, the problem is definitely your standards. If you can't increase your beauty naturally or find a venue where the type of men you prefer congregate, accept the average of all the men who wanted to *commit* to you in the past few years as a reflection of your value.

Consider how useful it is to gain the commitment of a man you know is not the highest status you could get: he will highly prize you and be less likely to cheat or leave. If I'm accustomed to dating girls who are a seven on a scale of one to ten, and suddenly a nine falls in love with me, I will probably never look at another girl again. I'm not advising you to marry a troglodyte, but there is value in dating a man who may be rough around the edges. At the very least, you should not chase after men whose value is so high that their interest in you will never go beyond the sexual. If a man has a stable job, has similar family values to yours, and you enjoy spending time with him in spite of his flaws, there isn't much more you can look for in a long-term partner.

Once you meet a man you like, the problem is getting him to ask you out. To avoid rejection, he may try the beta male method of becoming your friend and hoping that *you* will make the first move. My advice to men is to be bold, but I'm only one voice combating a chorus of cultural influences that are working to emasculate men. It doesn't help that many women harshly punish men when they try to strike up a conversation. Since a huge component of securing the commitment of a man is to have him invest in you, you should not ask a man out, just as you should not approach a man. The best thing you should do is to encourage a man with your body language and conversation while behaving like a lady.

If a man approaches you in a public venue, it is obvious that he is not a meek man, and he will definitely ask you for a date if he likes you. However, if you meet a man through a social circle or a community where he didn't have to approach you outright, he may hesitate to ask you out because he will be unsure if you like him. You can help to alleviate some of his doubt by encouraging him, but you should not remove all doubt to the point where he doesn't have to take any risk.

There are only two requirements for a man to ask you out. The first is for him to be attracted to you sexually. If a man is not attracted to you, it's game over, because your personality can never substitute for the physical. I know you don't want a man to desire you only sexually, but don't try to fight the hard truth that if you didn't have a vagina, you'd be in deep trouble. Embrace the fact that God has hard-wired men to appreciate a woman sexually first and foremost.

Secondly, a man won't ask a woman out unless he has a healthy level of confidence. If he doesn't possess an ounce of strength and is not willing to put himself out on the ledge to ask for a measly phone number, he is not man enough. I don't like to judge other men harshly, but there is no excuse for a grown man not to ask a woman out. I know of men with physical handicaps, such as deafness, who have the courage to ask women out, so I can't give a man who refuses to do this a pass. It's not your job to train a man to be a man—he should already know how to do the basics when he meets you.

To encourage a man to ask you out, give him *one* strategic compliment about his personality, humor, or intellect, but do not compliment his physical attractiveness, because it will make him think you primarily want sex. The compliment should make him excited that he has a chance with you. If he possesses sufficient testicular fortitude, he will prolong the conversation and eventually ask for your number.

Here are three examples of compliments you can give:

"It's nice for a change to meet someone who shares my beliefs."

"I don't usually meet men who have positive energy as you do."

"You think about things in an interesting way."

If you want to devise a compliment, make it pleasant, encouraging, and somewhat vague without implying an absolute guarantee that you will say yes if he asks you out.

Another way to encourage a man is to ask him personal questions apart from what he does for a living. Follow up on the personal stories or anecdotes he tells you. If he's talking about a recent trip he took, ask questions about it. If he's talking your head off about a certain kind of drink, ask about his interest in it. If he remarked that he likes to meditate, ask exactly how he meditates. When a man invests time in a specific topic, chances are it interests him greatly. Follow up with questions that encourage him to continue the conversation with you.

The end of a conversation is a do-or-die moment. Before this point, you gave multiple positive signs, including a strategic compliment, but the fear of rejection among men is so strong that it may be worth pushing him over the edge by saying the following: "I enjoyed this conversation with you." Say no more than that. If he *still* doesn't close the deal, you must pass. He's either not that attracted to you or not a masculine man. Going beyond this final statement would essentially be the same as asking him out, which is not your job. You cannot be both the woman and the man in a relationship.

If you do the work for a man in the beginning, you will have to do the work for him until the end. He will never step up. Encourage a man, respond to him, ask him questions, but don't chase him like you are the hunter. This may mean having to wait many months until a man who is ready to take a risk on you comes along, but it's better to wait than to put on the pants yourself and get into a relationship with a weak man you always have to lead.

A common scenario is wanting to eject from a conversation. You gave a man a shot but realized that he doesn't have the qualities you're looking for. I advise on the golden rule of treating him as you would like your brother or another male relative to be treated. When you're ready to go, simply say, "I'm sorry, but I have to go." It's helpful to add an excuse, such as being late for a meeting or needing to talk to your friends. If he asks for your number, say, "I'm sorry, but I'm not interested." Then turn around and withdraw from the interaction. If he persists, repeat your rejection word for word until he gets the message and gives up. The adult thing to do is to reject him in person instead of leading him on by giving him your number and then not responding when he calls or texts.

Even if your rejection is exceedingly polite, you will encounter men who get angry and say things such as "You're not hot anyway" or "Whatever, slut." This is especially common in nightclubs where alcohol is served. Men say these things because they are emotionally hurt by your rejection and want you to feel the pain that they're feeling. Don't take these insults personally, since a man doesn't know you well enough for them to be a reflection of who you really are. If you're regularly experiencing sour interactions at a particular venue, I advise you to go somewhere else, because you're probably in a hunting ground for men who just want to have fun.

When it comes to meeting men, the bottom line is to focus on your beauty and embrace your feminine core. This may be hard to do if you've been trained to chase, grab, and achieve, but it should be simple enough for you to turn off all these traits and become a passive ball of energy that is observing and evaluating the masculine energy that is attempting to come into you. If you like a man, encourage him with smiles, positive comments, strategic compliments, and follow-up questions. If he is indeed a man, he will act.

I've left many gaps unfilled when it comes to conversation, giving your phone number, and making plans, because it's the man's job to take the initiative while you either accept or reject his advances based on your feelings and level of interest. He's the driver and you're going along for the ride, and during that ride you will evaluate his driving skills and say yes or no while he strains to get you to like him. If he likes you and you like him, things will move into the realm of dating.

Dating

Depending on your perspective, dating is when the fun or the pain begins. Within one year of your journey, after improving your beauty, becoming more social, getting involved with communities, and moving slowly and invitingly in venues where men are present, you should rack up a significant number of interactions with men that lead to dates.

Before you have a first date, you may encounter men who exhibit two completely different types of behavior. The first type is men who do weird things from a place of neediness or anxiety. Examples of this are fishing for compliments, texting too quickly and expecting you to do the same, or anticipating you to take the lead on where to go for dates. If you believe the man has potential, gently tell him how you expect him to behave without emasculating him. Here are some examples of what you could say:

"I'm not used to a man who texts so quickly."

"I'd rather you pick the venue. I trust your judgment."

"You're putting too much pressure on me when you do that."

Unless a man is an experienced player, he's going to make many mistakes, especially in the early stages of the interaction. If you see redeeming qualities in him, it's best to be patient and see whether you can subtly hint how you expect him to behave.

The second type of behavior you'll encounter is a man pushing very quickly for sex while exhibiting other player traits. He'll try to sneak in a fast kiss, invite you to his apartment at the end of the first date (or earlier), send racy text messages requesting nude photos, and attempt to make last-minute plans that suggest he wants a booty call. I don't think I need to explain that these are signs he's only looking for physical pleasure.

Every single man you meet will want sex from you, but he should not flagrantly broadcast this fact. Remember that you will not be able to change a man's main motives or desires. The best you can do is nudge him ever so slightly in the right direction, but not substantially so. You will *always* fail to secure a relationship from a man who is feeding his devil.

On your first dates, I advise you to abstain from alcohol to weed out fun-stage men. Have tea, coffee, ice cream, or frozen yogurt instead. If a date asks why you don't drink, say that you do so only on "special occasions" and that there are "more downsides than upsides" to drinking. If you meet men in night venues, you'll have to abstain from drinking there as well to come across as consistent.

Men in their fun-stage know they have virtually no chance of attaining their goal of fast sex if a date doesn't drink. You're essentially flashing a bright red "I'm not easy" signal without actually having to say so. Once a man realizes you will be difficult, he'll get visibly stressed out and use all types of arguments in an attempt to persuade you to drink, perhaps even shaming you as "boring," but understand that the more he tries to get you to drink, the more likely he's just looking for a pump and dump.

You may be tempted to drink only one glass of wine, but one drink can easily turn into two, which will put you in danger of succumbing to temptation and breaking the two-ninths policy. Most women severely underestimate the effect that only one serving of alcohol has on their decision-making.

If I go on a date and a girl drinks, I put her in the promiscuous box and proceed accordingly, because I know that she has drunk alcohol around many men before, and what almost always follows drinking is casual sex. If I go on a date with a girl who doesn't drink, I start to consider her other qualities and whether she's a potential long-term partner, but unfortunately this rarely happens, and most girls I meet love to drink excessively. A man who is in settle-down mode will value you more highly when he discovers that you don't drink around men.

Your main complaint may be that it's impossible not to drink socially, and that I'm asking for way too much. You may be right, but the reason many women fail to enter relationships is that they date the wrong men, and this is largely because they are under the influence of alcohol in the early stages of dating.

When a man drinks alcohol, he gets exceedingly horny and will pass up the future wife for the easy girl. When a woman drinks alcohol, her devil is activated and pushes her to the sexy man with status instead of one who will protect and provide. Alcohol greatly impairs our ability to make good decisions and lowers our standards when deciding who to have sex with. If you like to drink and don't think you can live without it, I advise that you at least refrain from doing so around a man until you have sex with him. Otherwise, you will primarily attract fun-stage guys.

Understand that your behavior and not your words will tell a man everything he needs to know about you. If you drink heavily, share racy photos, and put out easily, why would he want more than sex from you? Saying that you're "not that type of girl" will fall on deaf ears. The point is that you're not trying to fake the qualities of a good girl— you *are* the good girl. You must shed any promiscuous behavior you've adopted from being born during the world's peak stage of degeneracy and embrace the positive side of your nature so you can bond with a man who is ready to settle down. Eliminating alcohol is a crucial step in accomplishing this goal.

In a promiscuous environment, men have learned to expect sex no later than the third date. Many may try way earlier. Too bad that they will have zero chance with you. Our two-ninths policy will cause them to see you as useless, a complete waste of time, while the settle-down man will see you as a potential wife. If a man really is ready to settle down, he will not eject before the ninth date, no matter how sexually frustrated he becomes. In fact, such a man will probably wait until marriage to have sex with the woman he sees as his ideal partner.

It's challenging for me to come up with a universal policy on sex for women who live in different parts of the world. For example, if you're from a small conservative town, kissing on date two and having sex on date nine may be seen as within the realm of normal and not at all hard for a man to endure. If you're living in New York City, on the other hand, the two-ninths policy will be exceptionally effective at blocking out fun-stage men. Assuming you live in a medium or large city, the two-ninths policy should provide a substantial delay that is likely to be the longest a man has ever encountered from a woman who is attracted to him. While it's fine to extend the timeline and delay intimacy even longer, I don't advise you to shorten it, which may happen unintentionally if you drink alcohol on dates.

If you're a virgin, you may be wondering if it's better to wait until marriage before having sex. I personally think that is a great idea, and I would consider marrying a virgin myself if the courtship wasn't longer than a year, but this is challenging to pull off if you're not embedded within a religious community. If you're not a virgin, however, delaying sex until marriage will come across as a charade.

Difficulties may arise if in the past you've slept with many random men. If I meet a girl today and she delays sex beyond a few dates, I will investigate her sexual history. In the case I find out that it's riddled with encounters where she put out quickly, I will drop out, because I will feel cheated if she denies me the physical satisfaction that she willingly gave other men who didn't put in as much time.

Imagine if a man insists on taking you to McDonald's for dinner on every date, telling you that he doesn't want to "waste" money on fine dining. Then you find out that he used to take dates to luxury Michelin-rated restaurants. You'd feel short-changed and think he cares less about you than the other girls he dated. A man feels the same way when it comes to sex.

You may be tempted to lie about your sexual history to overcome this problem. As I mentioned earlier, any lie will be exposed at some point, often when you least expect it, and erode the trust a man has in you to such an extent that he may end the relationship after you've invested a lot of time into it. Therefore, if you have engaged in promiscuous behavior and a man calls you out on trying to delay sex, you may lose him upon sharing the truth. This is a risk you must take.

At some point, you'll need a man to accept your past mistakes, just as you accept his, so I can't advise you to change the two-ninths policy even if a man thinks it's unfair, because if you do, you will return to the failed strategy of sleeping with men who aren't invested in you. You may have to give up on men who demand sex before date nine even if they seem like a good partner. Unless he can give you an ironclad pledge that he'll stick around if you break your rule for him, why should you do it?

While it's positive that you've learned from your past, you won't be able to escape it entirely. The more mistakes you've made, the more likely you will lose good men, just like how I've lost girls because of my public sexual history. That's the cost of living life. If it makes you feel better, you can blame the sick culture for your past behavior, because that's what I do!

Besides, if a man is putting intense pressure on you for sex, it may be a warning sign that he's in his fun stage. Don't think that succumbing to his pressure will ensure that he sticks around afterwards—it may do the exact opposite and accelerate his departure. The next man who loves you must accept that you've made mistakes and learned from them. If he sees you as a potential wife, he will be patient.

What's great about delaying sex for a long time is that you'll have nothing to be ashamed of when a man asks you about your sexual history. "I had sex with the last man I dated... on the ninth date... but it didn't work out." If a girl told me this, I definitely wouldn't put her in the fun box, because waiting that long for sex is almost unheard of. It's much better to get "burned" after ninth-date sober sex than to lose control on the first or second date while inebriated, well before you've had time to identify the values of a man and if he's dedicated to having a serious relationship.

Is it possible for the two-ninths policy to be too long and frustrating for even a good man? Understand that the number-one problem good men have isn't sex but finding a virtuous woman who doesn't sleep around. The fact that you don't drink and are not easy to get into bed will actually *excite* him into thinking that he has found a woman with the right values. There may be a problem if your sexual history is overly promiscuous, and you will have to disclose it at some point, but if you're buying a book like this, I imagine your sexual mistakes are minor compared with those of the general female population.

An additional benefit when a man accepts delaying sex is that you no longer have to ask yourself, "Does he like me?" A woman usually asks this question when she becomes physically intimate with a man quickly. Of course she's unsure whether he's just using her for sex when it was one of the first things they did together. When you offer a man fast sex and don't make him invest in you first, he will like you for sex and nothing else. This problem can easily be avoided by waiting nine dates before engaging in any kind of sexual activity. It provides you with evidence that yes, he does like you, yes, he is committing to you, and yes, sex won't be the primary feature of the relationship. Sex will be important, but the relationship will transcend beyond it.

You can identify how interested a man is more through his actions than his words. Unlike women, we don't like expressing our emotions. It's not that we don't feel, but others can use our feelings as a weapon to attack us. There's no need to get hung up on why a man is not regularly paying you compliments or verbally expressing his attraction for you as long as he's reliable and consistent. It would be nice if your man knows how to allay your insecurities, but most men don't have this ability because it's unnatural for a hunter to compliment the animal he's hunting before he has conquered her physically and spiritually. If a man chooses to be with you, that should be enough, and if you insist on forcing him to compliment you or express his feelings, he will come to resent you for it.

One additional concern you may have is that a player might stick around for nine dates only to pump and dump you. If a man is a genuine player, he is most likely to jump ship after the first date once he finds out that you don't drink or won't let him kiss you. If he has only a kiss to show for his efforts after hanging around for five dates, he will feel ashamed to tell his player friends that he has yet to get sex, and he will start pushing extra hard by inviting you straight to his apartment or insisting that you drink alcohol. At this point, you'll have all the information you need.

I've known more players than most men, but not a single one has waited until date nine or beyond, got sex, and then never contacted the girl again. I'm sure it has happened at some point in human history, but the odds of it happening are minuscule compared with the typical scenario of a girl drinking alcohol and having sex by the third date.

There are dozens of other details that are relevant when it comes to dating. How should you dress on dates? How quickly should you reply to his text messages or calls? How much interest should you show? What should you talk about? What should you do if he's not being assertive? What if he's behaving in a cheap manner? What if you catch him lying about something? What if he's becoming overly needy and creeping you out? Instead of trying to come up with a rehearsed response for every possible scenario, there are two overarching principles that you should keep in mind.

The first dating principle is to stick to your predetermined policy when it comes to intimacy while testing him to ascertain his real values. Do not succumb to his persistent demands for sex, and do not sacrifice your core need of wanting a man who is in his settle-down stage, ready to protect and provide. If you communicate these values, but a man is still far from acting on them, or simply doesn't get it, you have to abandon ship.

The second dating principle is to stay in the frame of him doing the hunting and you responding with encouragement and feminine energy. While it's fine to initiate text messages or suggest dates, it's his job to lead the interaction. This also means not trying to change his personality or habits. Every man is flawed, and during the initial nine dates you will have a good idea of what his flaws are. If his flaws are too big for you to handle, end the relationship. Otherwise, accept them, just as he should accept your flaws.

For example, let's say he's texting you a lot of silly things without asking out. How should you respond? The second principle kicks in, meaning you should withdraw from the interaction if he has had an opportunity to ask you out on a date but has failed to do so. It's not your job to be the masculine partner.

What if he's pushing hard for a kiss on the first date when you want to wait until date two? The first principle kicks in, which means you should tell him that it's too early. If he leaves, then great—you've just saved yourself from a potential pump-and-dump.

What if a man tells you he has a stable job but you discover he is unemployed with few future prospects? Since he is far from being able to protect and provide for his woman, the first principle kicks in, indicating that he's a poor choice. Lying is also a huge red flag that a man is in his fun stage and willing to say anything to get laid.

If you remind yourself of these two dating principles when an issue arises, you're more likely to make a good decision about what to do next.

The broken way to obtain a commitment is to date someone for an indeterminate amount of time while enjoying no-strings-attached sex and have the "talk" somewhere down the line. A woman who does this may be upset when she discovers that the man she likes, and with whom she has been having sex for months (or years), is not at all interested in monogamy or marriage, but this is to be expected, because why would a man want to take the relationship further when he's already comfortable and getting what he primarily wants? Such a woman will fail to get him to commit because she didn't pursue what she truly wanted or identify his values at the very beginning of the relationship.

The better option is to require a commitment to be monogamous, or be firm that sex will take place only once you're married. If you're going to ask for a commitment on date nine, make sure the man is of sober mind, because if he's sexually aroused, he'll agree to just about anything in order to get you into bed.

Won't you scare away a man if you require a commitment before sex? To answer this question, we have to ask what a man who is ready to settle down would do if he's dating a woman he cares about and sees as a potential wife. Would he be scared off on date nine when she states that she wants a commitment before she will sleep with him? No, he would not.

If tomorrow I meet a pretty girl who shares my values, is obviously not promiscuous, wants to sleep with me only, and sees me as a potential husband, I would be pleased with her suggestion, because the last thing I want to do with a potential wife is share her with other men. At the same time, I would agree only if I was *absolutely sure* we were a good match, which is likely to be the case if we made it to date nine without sex. If I were a woman, I'd want a strong assurance that a man is serious about me and would definitely seek a commitment before having sex. I would rather be burned by a man who breaks his commitment down the road than waste my time with one who never intended to commit in the first place. (In a few pages, I will discuss how to secure a man's commitment.)

Since you now have a screening process that mercilessly excludes fun-stage men, I expect you not to experience many failures after having sex. Your biggest problem will be that very few men will make it to date nine. This won't be a surprise, because as I've discussed, most men are in their fun stage, and even many men in their settle-down stage won't feel highly compatible with you, through no fault of your own. Taking my advice means you will need more willpower not to have sex with men you are sexually attracted to but who don't have any long-term potential. This may mean going long periods without sex, to the point where your female friends implore you to sleep with anyone to break your cold streak. If you listen to them, you will feel guilty after a meaningless sexual encounter and not be any closer to finding the man you want.

Depending on the quality of men in your city, along with its population size, it may take up to two years to enter a committed relationship with a man you're highly compatible to. I know this is not what you want to hear, especially in a culture that promises quick results, but understand that the kind of man you're looking for is either already in a relationship or lost in a sea of men who are just trying to get laid. Even worse is that you won't experience "mini-successes" along the way to stay encouraged, which means you will fail to make it to the critical sex stage with more than 99% of the men you meet before finally succeeding with one. You may feel like a nun at times, and you will certainly be teased by friends.

I advise that you wait at least six months before lowering your standards. The clock should start running once you've improved your appearance and begun displaying yourself to potential men through social circles, community networks, and public venues. If you're finding it difficult to meet good men after six months, the problem may be that you are stuck in the frame of wanting to feel sexually attracted to a man when you meet him. Without even realizing it, you're dismissing men who don't create a good first impression. I understand that you don't want to marry an "ugly" man or one who is unkempt, but you need to probe deeper when you meet men you don't have an instant attraction for to see whether they have values that are not visible on the surface.

For example, let's say I see a pretty girl at an outdoor café who's wearing a revealing shirt and smoking a cigarette. Off the bat, I want to dismiss her as promiscuous, but because she meets my beauty standards, I decide it's worth having a conversation with her to find out what kind of person she is. If she tells me that she's trying to quit smoking because her priest advised her to and that she's wearing her sister's "awful" shirt because it's laundry day, I may consider her for a date. The point is not to write off someone immediately if they present yellow flags instead of red ones. If a girl has tattoos and facial piercings, which are definitely red flags for men in their settle-down stage, I would not have a chat with her.

If you've been feeding your devil for your entire life, it's to be expected that you won't be interested in good men who put out a protector and provider vibe. Your negative perceptions are based on your habits and experiences, not on objective standards of what a good man is. This is why I advise waiting at least six months before you start to widen your funnel for more men to enter it, because the problem may not be the men you're meeting but that your devil is sabotaging how you view them. Stick to your guns so that your devil weakens enough for you to develop healthier attraction instincts. As long as a man has a decent job and is obviously not in his fun stage, you should give him a chance, even if your first impression of him is not entirely favorable. Set aside snap judgments about his appearance and behavior to look deeper into his values.

A warning sign that you may have to do some serious soul searching is if men in their settle-down stage are consistently passing you up. If you're meeting a number of men who are hungry for a wife, but they are not choosing you, it's possible that you are not putting out feminine signals of love, nurturing, and selflessness. Are you presenting yourself as career-oriented? Does your behavior come across as bossy or masculine? Do your stories imply that you're maintaining a fun lifestyle? If you refuse to embrace the feminine, the masculine will not want to embrace you.

If you're having a rough time after one year, you may start thinking of moving or traveling. This isn't a bad idea for men because women in third-world countries are more conservative, and travel taps into our innate masculine spirit of exploration and conquest, but it's still an exceedingly difficult option that can take years to yield meaningful results. Apart from short trips for fun, I wouldn't advise a man to go "wife hunting" abroad unless he has completely exhausted all other avenues for meeting women in his home country.

In your case, I don't advise moving or traveling at all, mainly because it is time-consuming. Since your biological clock is ticking much faster than a man's, you can't afford to waste years trying to find men in faraway cities or countries who may differ only superficially from the men in the city or town where you live. In addition, foreign men will always view you as easy pickings because of the stereotype that Western women are the most promiscuous in the world. You will attract way more men in their fun stage than in your home city.

Traveling makes sense only if you meet a foreign man in your home city or town and decide to move to his hometown in order to have a family. Otherwise, travel will simply feed your devil. You'll become caught up in a routine of seeking novelty, taking exciting selfies, and meeting men with sexy accents who seem to be fawning over you and saying romantic things, but who primarily see you as a release for their sexual needs, quickly disappearing once you suggest commitment.

Single And Over 30

Things become more complicated if you're 30 or older. You're running out of time to meet a man, fall in love, go through an engagement period, get married, and have children before it becomes biologically difficult to do so. It doesn't help that you're past your peak in terms of beauty and don't get as much attention from men as you did when you were younger. Your standards are also the highest they have ever been due to your past experiences, which makes matters worse because most attractive men who meet your standards will regard your declining beauty and fertility as negatives. Ideally, you do not want to be single after the age of 30, but if you find yourself in this situation, I have two pieces of advice.

First, you have to lower your standards *substantially*, to a level you once would have regarded as insane. That laundry list of qualities a man should have? Burn it. At this point, you should be solely seeking a man with good values. This means you will have to try out men who are of below-average appearance or have a personality that is borderline "weird." You must immediately pass on more attractive men who are clearly in their fun stage and only want to have sex with you. Place sexual attraction on the backburner.

Secondly, you should focus on men who are at least five years older than you, preferably closer to ten. The reason is that an older man will greatly value you as a younger, fresher, and more fertile catch. It is also more likely that these men will be in their settle-down stage since they can hear their own biological clock ticking. Contrary to what mainstream culture says, most normal men love younger women, and you should use this to your advantage.

The biggest mistake I see women older than 30 make is dating younger men. These pairings have an extremely high failure rate because it is virtually guaranteed that younger guys are in their fun stage and looking to have sex with a "mature woman." When I was in my mid-twenties, it was easier to have sex with girls in their late twenties and early thirties, because girls in their early twenties receive so much attention from men that they tend to be flakier and harder to get out on a date. Horny men choose the path of least resistance to achieving their sexual goals, which means that they see older women as a source of easy sex, *not* relationships. Instead, go in the other direction. Find a man who is moderately older than you and looking to beat his biological clock at the same time you're trying to beat yours.

Another benefit of an older man is that his energy and testosterone will be lower. He'll be less likely to cheat or spend his nights getting drunk with his friends. A potential downside is that he will be stuck in his ways and have strange habits. Every man is different, and you'll have to screen all of them carefully regardless of age, but one who is five to ten years older than you will value you as a potential wife significantly more than a man of your age or younger. A 40-year-old man will truly feel like he won the lottery if he's dating a 30-year-old woman who has maintained her appearance, and he will be far more likely to commit to her.

The last thing a woman wants to hear is that she should lower her standards and date a man who is potentially unattractive, but if you're single and over 30, you don't have many other options. Because it takes such a long time to go from being single to having a child, even in ideal circumstances, you need to adjust your standards significantly or risk failing to become a mother.

It's not fair that you have a shorter biological clock than men, but you have to accept this reality and make changes accordingly, starting today. If you don't want to be a mother, that's fine, but if it's something you strongly desire, you have to act quickly. As long as a man you meet has good values and sees you as a prize, you have more than enough to move forward into a relationship. From this point on, forget about all the sexy men who give you attention—now you know they just want sex. It's time to look for a mature man who is ready for commitment, marriage, and fatherhood.

So far, I've covered how to meet a man and what to do up to the first time you have sex. The last part of the book will focus on securing a commitment and sustaining a healthy relationship.

LADY

Book III: Relationships

I'm extremely skeptical of anyone who claims to be a "relationship expert." Either that person has had a number of failed relationships, and is likely to have more, or he has had only one successful relationship, which gives him a whopping sample size of one. If I create one successful business, am I a business expert? If I make one woman orgasm continually, am I a sex expert? I absolutely do not claim to be a relationship expert, though I have been hyper-aware of what worked and didn't work in my failed relationships.

I have also become a node through which hundreds of people, both men and women, have shared their dating and relationship stories. I've noticed enough patterns to provide you with an ideal relationship solution that works within the context of modern culture.

I do think traditional ways are best for long-term relationships, but achieving this in a non-traditional age is impossible, and most of us have not lived anything that remotely resembles a traditional life. We must therefore arrive at a compromise that takes from what has worked in the past while accounting for the contemporary environment that continually feeds the devils within us.

Commitment

Most women see commitment as a process that unfolds gradually. You meet a man, you like him, you sleep with him, you date him for a while, you agree to commit, and the relationship escalates with the intention of eventually getting married. It's what most of your friends do and what you've seen in movies since you were young.

For a man, the decision on whether or not to commit is based on logic. He asks himself what he will gain by making a commitment or escalating the relationship. If a man only wants sex, primarily because he's in his fun stage, what will he gain through a commitment? If he's already having sex, nothing. If a man wants a girlfriend to alleviate loneliness or have someone to hang out with, what will he gain through a commitment? Nothing as well, because his needs are already being met through a casual relationship. Men agree to a commitment mainly so that they will *not lose* what they're already getting. Their motives are based on avoiding a negative (lack of sex, loneliness) instead of achieving a positive (family). The problem is that a man has little motivation to get married if it's merely to avoid experiencing pain.

Most men simply want sex, and since women give them sex freely when dating, a man will balk at his woman's attempt to secure a commitment. She will complain to friends that her boyfriend is a man-child who hasn't grown up, whereas the reality is that she is already providing him with everything he wants. This is why it's essential to determine a man's values before sex to find out if he wants more than a casual relationship, because you cannot make a man want something that he hasn't already decided he wants.

From a man's perspective, committing to you has only two benefits. First, it prevents you from sleeping around (assuming you don't cheat). Many men do not want to share their woman with other men. The second benefit is that a commitment is the most rational step before having a family. It is likely that a man who wants children will want them to be raised within a stable family environment, which requires a man and a woman to make a vow, first informally as a promise and then in court and possibly before God. By selecting for men in their settle-down stage who want children with a devoted wife, you'll find it far easier to get a commitment than your friends who don't screen a man's values at all before going to bed with them.

It will not work if you withhold certain benefits and bestow them only if your man agrees to make a commitment. For example, if you tell a man that you cook or clean only for serious boyfriends, he will resent you and see you as manipulative. Consider how you would feel if a man said, "I only introduce serious girlfriends to my friends, not girls I'm merely having sex with." You'd be hurt that he was withholding something in order to get you to do something else.

The better approach is to be the ideal partner from day one for the man who knows he wants to marry the ideal partner. In that case, he'll rush to take you off the dating market and make you his wife within three years. A man will either want a future with you or he will not, and trying to micro-manage or manipulate him into monogamy will fail in the end.

If a man sees you as a potential wife, he'll want to secure a commitment relatively early. He may raise the subject indirectly by asking about the other men you know and what their intentions are, and will say he doesn't think it's a good idea for you to spend time with them. A feminist may state that such a man is "controlling," "jealous," or "over-protective," but the reality is that if he doesn't care about the other men in your orbit, he will never settle down with you. Either something is wrong with his protect-and-provide instinct or he's spending time with other women.

I admit that I'm firmer than the average man when it comes to what I expect from a girl who wants a commitment, mostly because of my extensive experience with promiscuous women. I've noticed firsthand how impulsive women can be, how easily they will cheat (particularly if they consume alcohol), and how adept they are at lying in the face of objective evidence to the contrary. Therefore, I expect my woman not to have one-on-one meetings with men, not to have long conversations with them (whether online or offline), and not to travel for fun without me or family members. I have a high tolerance for a woman who is overly emotional or throws temper tantrums, but practically no tolerance for her having relationships with other men, because this can lead to infidelity and the dissolution of the relationship.

If I identify a girl who is perfect for me, but she doesn't agree to my standards, I will not continue the relationship, because experience has taught me that a girl who doesn't meet my standards is not ready to be my wife. Most men are less experienced than me when it comes to knowing the true nature of women, so I expect their standards to be lower, but if a man's standards are too low, it could be a sign that he is not serious about the relationship or is disconnected from his masculine instinct. It's essential that a man demonstrates he has standards to indicate that he is invested in the relationship and wants it to last for the rest of his life.

I advise men to wait for the girl to raise the issue of commitment first, because it helps us to gauge the status of the relationship. If I've been sleeping with a girl for a couple of months and she doesn't raise the subject, I assume she doesn't want a relationship with me and doesn't care if I sleep around since she's doing it herself. It makes no sense for me to disturb an arrangement based on sex by seeking a commitment from a girl who is simply using me for my body. This is especially the case if it wasn't hard for me to get her into bed and her sexual history suggests that she has been with dozens or hundreds of men.

The most natural way for you to bring up commitment is after he shares an anecdote about a woman. Ask him if he's seeing other women. Then say that you value your relationship with him and are ready to take it to the next level because you are not seeing another man and have no desire to. If he sees you as his future wife, he will be pleased—but not necessarily visibly excited—at what you said and be inclined to agree once he has communicated what he expects from you in a relationship. Commitment is a big step for a man, even if he's falling in love with a girl, so don't take it the wrong way if he doesn't jump for joy at the idea.

If a man is certain that you won't be his future wife, he'll resist the idea of commitment by declining outright or saying that he's "not ready." Understand that if a man says he's not ready, what he's really saying is that he's not ready *for you*, ever, because a man is always ready for his ideal girl, even if sex has yet to take place. This bad news will be unpleasant to hear, but the upside is that you will know for certain that the relationship is dead.

A response that tends towards the negative is when he asks for "more time" to think it over. A man is likely to use this line if you caught him off guard, meaning he hadn't considered a relationship with you. Give him a couple of weeks to think it over before bringing up the topic again, but expect his answer to still be "not ready."

I advise that you have the commitment talk no later than two months after you have sex with a man. There are three reasons for this. First, it's still early enough for him not to have become so sedated with "free sex" that it becomes all he wants from you. Second, it's more than enough time for him to develop feelings for you. Third, you won't have wasted too much of your time if it turns out that he was simply using you for sex.

Remember that sex is a man's number-one need, so unless he is specifically looking to create a family, he will do everything possible to keep the relationship solely in the realm of sex. If he does refuse to commit, your best option is to break up with him, take a break for a few weeks, and then dive back into the dating market to meet another man.

If you want to gain a man's commitment before having sex with him, he will agree only if his head is screwed on right and he knows exactly what he wants. This is your safest option, and I *strongly* recommend it, but it's guaranteed to fail unless you're absolutely sure the man is in his settle-down stage and both of you are highly compatible. If a man is merely leaning towards settling down but is not firmly there, he will probably reject a commitment before sex unless he's so horny that he'll agree to give you one of his kidneys just to sleep with you.

Getting a proposal of marriage is a bigger challenge than a commitment to monogamy, because most men are aware of the destructive nature of marriage laws and the family courts. Even though I genuinely want a family, I'm hesitant about signing a legal contract that comes with a monumental set of downsides that could result in my financial ruin or even imprisonment, a concern that is shared by just about all the men I know. By now, I hope you can see that the more victories that feminists achieve, the less likely a man will be eager to marry you. Whenever you see a hairy-legged lesbian feminist push for more stringent laws that will further reduce the number of men who will want to get married, it may be a good idea to speak out against her.

The best thing you can do to make a man excited at the prospect of marriage is to minimize his financial risk by agreeing to a prenuptial agreement. You may see this as tacky, but it alleviates most of the anxiety a man has about marriage, particularly if he has a high income. There is remaining risk for a man even if you do sign a prenup, but it shouldn't stop a man who is determined to start a family. On the other hand, if a man is not sure whether he wants to be a father, he will refuse to marry even if you agree to sign a prenup. Seeking a man who has decided to have children before you meet him is the best indication that he will go all the way with you in spite of the risks.

The problem with most women is that they have absolutely no screening process and are shocked by their "bad luck" when they experience failed relationship after failed relationship. Personally, I can't remember the last woman who asked my opinion on family life and children before she had sex with me. It's even worse when a woman asks a man about having a family a *year* or more after entering a relationship with him. This won't happen to you. Screen a man from the first date, stick to the two-ninths policy, and terminate interactions with men who are not in their settle-down stage.

Within one year of a relationship, you'll have experienced virtually every aspect of your man's personality and gained insight into his values, thanks to spending long periods in his company through sleepovers or short vacations. You want to know him well enough by the end of the first year to be able to provide a definitive "Yes" or "No" to the question, "Do I want to have a family with him?" To help you answer, have discussions about children and how you think they should be raised. For example, I'm sympathetic to homeschooling and would ask my girlfriend if she can see herself doing it. I may also ask her opinion about the negative effects of electronic devices on children, adding that I don't want my kids to use tablets. There should be a general agreement on how you both approach child-raising.

By the first anniversary of a committed relationship, you want a full picture of who he is, what he's like to live with, and what kind of father he'd be. If you're satisfied with that picture, start dropping hints about marriage, perhaps by relating anecdotes about friends or relatives who are getting married. Gauge his reaction to the idea. If he's hesitant about marriage, find out what his objections are. If they're related to his concerns about divorce, say you're willing to sign a prenup. If they're related to his need for personal space, demonstrate that you can respect his boundaries by reading books or busying yourself with other things while you're at his place.

As long as his objections don't conflict with your core values, make an effort to squash them in the next two or three months. Then raise the topic of marriage again. Does he have any objections this time? If he does, try to resolve them once more. If he doesn't have any objections, give him time—but not too much time—to arrive at the decision to ask you to marry him, without presenting him with an ultimatum.

By the second anniversary, you want him to have proposed marriage or have come extremely close to doing so. Modern couples often take longer than two years to get married, but remember that you don't have unlimited time. You don't want to waste more than two years with a man who is not serious about marrying you, because you may need this time to search for another man. If you're older than 30, you may want to shorten the time from two years to eighteen months or even less.

Another reason not to wait longer than two years is that the passion and sexual attraction will naturally fade as you get into years three and four. Unless you have children to cement the bonds of love, you run the risk of becoming bored with each other and going your separate ways. Children will be necessary as the passion fades to transform the relationship into a pair-bond that lasts for decades.

You may ask if you should marry a man you're not in love with. The problem is that many women confuse love with lust and sexual excitement. Even the notion of romantic love is flawed because it's primarily based on emotion, which changes and fades over time, instead of values, which are more constant and stable. All emotional butterflies eventually disappear, and if there are no values behind those butterflies, there is no need for a relationship to continue.

If your idea of a loving relationship is based on something out of a Hollywood movie, you're chasing an illusion and will fail with marriage. On the other hand, if it's based more on mutual values, pair-bonding, and creating a loving family home, you will succeed. Movies and romance novels are fictional and do not portray relationships that withstand the test of time. Holding up these fictions as the ideal of love and using them to decide if you should marry a man will certainly cause you to pursue men who will fail in their commitments to you.

We also have to account for the influence of your devil. Does he really want you to be with only one man? Does he really want you to create a family? Of course not. Your devil wants you to have fun and get back on the treadmill of seeking novelty, money, and high-status men. He will aggressively put doubts in your mind and try to convince you that the man you're seeing is wrong for you because you aren't feeling any butterflies. He will try to drag you back on the loveless dating carousel because being with one man is too boring for him.

A man's devil operates in a similar way. He tells us to go back to banging promiscuous girls because it's fun and will make us feel more masculine. He tells us that marriage is slavery and it's better to be alone, and that the woman we're in love with will probably cheat on us anyway.

Let your devil's thoughts flow through you without acting on them. He will get tired after a few days or weeks and leave you alone for a while. When he does return, he will be weaker because you didn't feed him previously. Unless your partner is waving bright-red flags that indicate he will not be a good husband, or his views on child-rearing contradict yours, you must interpret your doubts as groundless and let them harmlessly run their course.

Another reason you may be doubtful about marrying a good man is if you're an alpha widow. If you had a short-term relationship with a very high-status man in the past, your devil will convince you that you can land a man of equal or greater status today. The problem is that the high-status man wasn't a good prospect to begin with because he never intended to marry you, so it doesn't make sense to compare him with a man who *is* willing to marry you. Don't confuse your ability to attract men for sex with your ability to attract a man who wants to commit.

Instead of focusing on the downsides of marrying a man you don't lust after, consider the upsides of stability and comfort. If you take my advice and find a man who sees you as a prize, he will dedicate himself to you and be resistant to straying. Any resulting marriage is sure to last. You will not have the roller-coaster emotions, the passionate fights, or the I-almost-passed-out sex, but if you do experience these things, you're with a man who almost certainly doesn't value stability and marriage. You can't have it both ways. Choosing one outcome will lead to a lonely life with only a career, pets, and casual sex to keep you occupied, whereas the other will lead to a family with a husband and children to love.

I don't buy the "I don't settle" argument that many women have. Since there is no such thing as a perfect man who can fulfill all of your desires, you're technically "settling" with every man you date, guaranteeing that each one will have at least one major habit, belief, or physical flaw that you'd rather he not have. Declaring that you "won't settle" is a self-defense mechanism that helps you to conceal your failures in relationships, which are more about sacrifice and trade-offs than refusing to depart an inch from an imaginary standard, something which I often have to remind myself of.

Maintenance And Care

Most of the time, you will find that a monogamous relationship is relaxing, mundane, and loving. I do not advocate using any techniques or strategies to sustain your relationship—simply allow your natural pair-boding instinct to take over. Connect with your man, show him the totality of your personality, and be generous with your rapport and love.

Once the commitment is secure and the relationship stabilizes, you'll have fewer worries than you did when you were single. As long as you keep in mind that your biological clock is ticking and that he should propose marriage within two years, there's nothing else for you to stress about. I'll now share some general guidelines on how a man likes to be treated by the woman he thinks he could marry.

It's actually easier to explain how we *don't* want to be treated. We don't want you to treat us like we're one of your co-workers. A relationship based on love is not the same as one based on making money or widgets, so avoid speaking or behaving in a professional, detached, and indirect way as you would when dealing with staff in the workplace. Keep the passive-aggressive politicking in the office.

You're not our equal when it comes to leadership of the household. Your role is equal in the sense that you comprise 50% of the basis of the relationship and 50% of its importance, but when it comes to leadership, your man comprises at least 90%. Leadership is compatible with the masculine side of his nature, while submission is compatible with the feminine side of yours, but this doesn't mean that he's the master and you're the slave. A leader must have the respect and consent of those he leads. You must believe that your boyfriend's arguments and actions are correct or you will start to question his leadership and act out in subversive ways. A leader has a great responsibility to be righteous, and if your man continually leads you into misfortune or disaster, you have every right to doubt him or even leave. It's a huge responsibility to direct other people's lives, but as a man, I don't have a choice because women—particularly feminine women—will not respect me if I don't lead.

Treat your man as the captain of the ship and give him the benefit of the doubt when he makes a decision that you may not entirely agree with. Focus on the outcome of his past decisions as a way to calm your fears or doubts when he makes a new decision. Did his previous decisions help to strengthen the relationship? Did they eventually improve your situation in life? Unless they clearly didn't, there should be no reason to doubt him.

I understand that it's hard for you to treat a man as the captain of your life after being programmed to be a big boss who seeks to conquer the world through masculine ambition, but a healthy relationship will endure only if there are one masculine leader and one feminine follower. You simply cannot have two chefs in the kitchen. It's possible for the roles to be reversed, where the woman takes on the masculine role and the man takes on the feminine role, but this works only with women who are biologically masculine from having high levels of testosterone.

At the very least, do not complain about his decisions unless you have a rock-solid logical argument of why they are wrong, or when you feel that it's *obvious* the ship is heading for a massive iceberg that he simply can't see. However, you'll find that your concerns almost never come to fruition, and if they do, your man will harshly punish himself for it on his own. Let him learn from his mistakes and acquire the experience he needs to make better decisions in the future. Nagging him, or rubbing his face in a bad decision by saying "I told you so" will breed resentment and lay the foundation for explosive conflict in the future.

Because a man is driven more by logic than emotion, he will instinctively be motivated to seek stability. A woman's emotions tend to sabotage stability, especially if they come from her devil and not her angel. This is why a man is less likely to listen to you when he feels your objections are driven by your emotions. Your emotions are important to your feminine essence, especially when raising children, but when it comes to your man making decisions, be deferential instead of challenging. Assume that he knows best. If he makes a mistake, which is inevitable because he's human, give him the opportunity to correct it. He will love you even more for your patience and understanding.

In fact, consider yourself lucky that you've found a man who is prepared to lead at all. The modern male often fears being assertive or masculine, and may want you to lead instead. This may seem great at first, because no decision will be made without your approval, but it will undoubtedly lead to misery. The extra responsibility will make you stressed and worn out as it clashes head-on with a feminine core that does not want to lead.

In a case of "Be careful what you wish for," feminists have achieved their goal of empowerment and realized that it's not what they wanted. Trying to lead makes their lives harder because it forces them to adopt an unnatural masculine role to deal with constant struggles and difficulties rather than allowing a strong man to deal with them instead. Even I'm not particularly enthusiastic about having to take responsibility for a woman's life, but at least it's compatible with my masculine essence.

At the end of the day, I know that if I create a stable environment for a woman, she will probably get used to the stability and take it for granted, causing her to occasionally challenge me for no reason, but if I make big mistakes that definitely hurt the relationship, I won't hear the end of it, and she may leave me. Therefore, it's in my best interests to make good decisions for the woman I love.

A better alternative to challenging your man's authority outright is to gently relay your concerns. Calmly share your opinion with him so that he's made aware of any potential downsides. For example, imagine your man is thinking of changing jobs to work for a smaller company. Instead of telling him what he should or shouldn't do, relay your concerns: "I'm only nervous that a smaller company is more likely to go out of business and put you out of work." When making his decision, he will take your opinion into account without feeling resentment towards you.

Another example is if he's having a problem with his health but doesn't want to go to the doctor. Instead of demanding that he goes, say, "It's probably nothing, but I'm concerned it will become a bigger problem if you don't have it checked out. I can make an appointment with the doctor if you like." Here you are gently sharing your opinion with him and making an offer to help instead of nagging or commanding him. Whichever decision he makes, you must respect him for it, and if turns out that you were right, do not rub it in. This will humiliate him and bruise his ego.

Ultimately, it's his decision on where to work or how he should take care of his body. You may not be pleased with those decisions, but you will create more problems if you try to force him to do what you want him to do. If he asks you directly for your input or advice, feel free to be more upfront, but if he doesn't, refrain from doing more than sharing your concerns without being emotional or con-demning him. If he wanted a nagging mother, he would probably still be living with his own, so aim to speak to him as if he's the captain of the ship and you're the first mate. When you calmly provide your input instead of issuing orders, I guarantee he'll at least take your views into account when deciding what to do.

Don't feel chafed if he implements your suggestion and then takes all the credit for the outcome. It may be hard for him to admit that you were right, but as long as there's a favorable outcome for the household, there's no need to point out that you upstaged him. Let his ego have a public victory while yours has a private one.

A major key to a successful relationship is understanding that a man needs significantly more "alone time" than you do to process his thoughts, make sense of his existence, and relieve stress. The number-one complaint I hear from men in relationships is that their girlfriends constantly require them to act the clown and be a source of entertainment as if they were a human television. Even when a man tells his girl that he needs space, she'll give it to him for only a few days or weeks, not understanding that his need for space is permanent.

The late comic Patrice O'Neal called women "time vampires," implying that they derive more energy from spending time with men than from having sex with them. On the other hand, most men replenish their energy when they are *away* from women. You may think something is wrong with your relationship if your man says that he needs to be alone, because you find it uncomfortable to be alone yourself, but he has completely different wiring than you. Once he has had sufficient alone time, he will be full of energy and seek you out. You will drain his energy again, prompting the need for another recharge. Don't feel insulted that men generally see women as a drain, because we would rather you consume our energy than anything else.

Our solitary nature should not be confused with a lack of interest. Men want to be alone but not lonely. We want you to be around us, but not necessarily in the same room talking to us. The best way to accomplish this is to have something you can do by yourself when you're with your man. One of my ex-girlfriends was a voracious reader, so she would always have a book in her hand when coming over. Whenever she sensed that I needed my alone time, she would relax on the bed or couch and read without bothering me.

It will almost always be the case that your man needs to interact with you less than you need to interact with him, and when he notices that you won't be a time vampire, he'll start seeing you as an ideal wife who grants him his much-needed alone time to read, work, or do things you may view as senseless, such as watching conspiracy videos on the internet or investing in cryptocurrency.

Another important thing to understand is that a man's testosterone decreases when he's in a long-term relation-ship, particularly one that is older than a year. Testosterone is a hormone that nature gave to men so we can hunt for food and women, but if a man is committed to you, he no longer has to hunt. As a result, his testosterone decreases significantly, lowering his vigor and sex drive to the point where he won't initiate sex with you as often as he did in the past. He essentially becomes a happy zoo animal ready for his scheduled "sex feedings," but this will cause you to think he's losing interest, unlike how he was early in the relationship when he couldn't wait to devour you. Even worse, your man may open the door for his devil to put thoughts into his mind of sleeping with other women, not because he doesn't love you, but because he wants to feel like a hunter again.

If he's fantasizing about having sex with other women, it's likely his fantasies will involve women who have qualities that you don't have. If you're a brunette, he will fantasize about blondes. If you have big boobs and a small butt, he will fantasize about a girl with small boobs and a big butt. The devil greatly values novelty, so he will try to convince your man that hunting someone who is complete-ly different than you will bring him happiness.

Give him that novelty yourself. Experiment in the bedroom with sexy outfits, dirty talk, role-playing, and different-colored wigs. Wear a short skirt in public so that he's aroused and can't wait to get you home. Put on a revealing schoolgirl outfit while you cook a meal for him so that he forgets about eating. Wear a wig and put on makeup so that you look completely different.

To keep a man sexually interested, trigger his hunting instinct by randomly giving him erotic sex. This will trick his devil into thinking that he did sleep with a completely new girl. You'll know it's time to try something spicy when he's initiating sex far less frequently than when the relationship started or when you sense he's checking out other women.

An even stronger way to maintain his sexual interest is to improve your appearance as the relationship progresses instead of allowing it to degrade. A man will definitely lose physical interest in you if you gain weight. He may not complain about it, because he doesn't want to make you upset, but you won't find a single man in the universe who states that he's satisfied with his girlfriend gaining weight. Not only will he lose attraction for you, but he'll start to visualize how many extra pounds you'll gain during the marriage, since it's exceedingly common for weight gain to accelerate after the wedding.

You should also keep your hair long. Unfortunately, many women start shortening their hair after gaining a man's commitment. To save a minute or two a day on hair care, they sabotage their relationship by getting old-lady cuts. If anything, a relationship is when you should test how long you can grow your hair. Increasing your beauty as the relationship progresses is not only a way to make your man proud of you, but it also tells him that you won't let yourself go, as many women do. Men don't suddenly lose their visual and aesthetic sense when they fall in love.

The final thing that will prove to him that you will make a good wife is not to cheat on him or put yourself in situations that *could* lead to cheating. If I have a girlfriend who continually wants to meet her single girlfriends or male "friends" in venues that serve alcohol, I know she is halfway towards cheating on me, if not already doing so. In such an environment, it won't be hard for a man to finagle an intimate conversation or dance with her, or even sneak in a kiss.

Hanging around men who will sleep with you if given the chance is the same as inviting a recovering alcoholic to a raging New Year's Eve party at a nightclub. To stay faithful, you'll have to say no to situations that could tempt you to access new men or seek the intimate attention of male "friends" who obviously want more than friendship by mere sake of being male.

Nothing bad can happen if you avoid situations that could turn bad. If a woman constantly puts herself in bad situations, I have to assume she's ready to do bad things and is therefore not a good prospect for marriage. To avoid dangerous situations that could spontaneously activate your devil, don't spend time alone with a man and avoid hanging out with promiscuous girlfriends at places that serve alcohol. Go out with all the men and party girls you want while you're single, but this should stop when you're in a relationship so that you can build a high level of trust with your man. If you have some kind of addiction to male attention, work it out of your system before you tell a man that you want a commitment, because if you don't, chances are you will burn him and waste both his time and yours.

Men are increasingly skeptical of girls who claim they have male "friends" when they have probably used the friendship tactic themselves to get inside a girl's pants. If at least one party in a friendship is sexually interested in the other, which is true 99% of the time with the man wanting to sleep with the woman, what you have is not a friendship but an extended courtship.

Imagine what would happen right now if you sent a text message to all the male friends in your phone that says, "Hey, I'm feeling lonely today. Can you come over with a bottle of wine at 10pm?" At 9:59pm, there would be a queue of excited men outside your front door. Instinctively, women know that their male friends would have sex with them if they could, but women—and their devils—love the fawning attention, so they maintain the charade that these men are only "friends" who have no sexual interest in them. I refuse to tolerate this sham, along with many men who are serious about settling down. If you want to have a lot of male friends, stay single, but don't try to deceive a man who is ready to take the next step.

Just as important as limiting contact with horny men and staying faithful is not lying. The problem with lying, apart from being immoral, is that when a lie is discovered, it drastically erodes trust in the relationship, and once trust is gone, the relationship is poisoned. It may seem easy to tell your man a few lies today, but he will discover them in due time, and when he does, he'll wonder what other lies you might have told him, and he won't believe anything you say in the future. Lies about the other men you know or your sexual history are especially damaging because a man can't help but start to question your fidelity. If this happens, it will be impossible for him to see you as a potential wife.

Men are also increasingly becoming aware of the tactics women use to cover up their misdeeds. For example, when a woman is putting herself in a position to cheat, she'll start acting jealous or accuse her man of cheating to deflect the heat from herself. I once had a girlfriend get furious with me for watching a YouTube video of a fully clothed girl doing a sexy dance. I later found out that she was conceal-ing the extent of her relationship with a male "friend," which was far worse than me watching a non-pornographic video clip. Putting pressure on me was a way for her to relieve the guilt of her impropriety, but it gave me a clue to examine her behavior more closely.

Not every man is a human lie detector like me, but the lies that are discovered begin to drain the life out of a relationship. If you're only interested in casual relationships, things will probably end before any of your lies are discovered, but when it comes to life-long relationships, the truth will be exposed at a gigantic cost when you least expect it.

The last important feature of maintaining your relationship is to take care of his home, or if you live together, your shared home. Remember that a man wants a woman who makes his life easier when it comes to cooking and cleaning. In exchange, we'll sacrifice our lives for yours and eternally protect and provide for you. That's a pretty good deal!

Early in the relationship, you won't be doing much homemaking, but as you start spending more nights at his place, you'll have the opportunity to make him drinks, cook, and tidy up around the house. If you move into his place (the verdict is out if this is a good idea before marriage), you should be doing most of the cooking and cleaning. The more homemaking you do, the more he'll see you as a wife, unlike the booty-call girl who comes over, has sex, and leaves the place in worse shape than it was before she arrived.

A sign that I have a keeper on my hands is when a girl picks up her dishes after spending time in my home for the first time. If she's making me clean up after her at such an early point in the relationship, when she should be trying to impress me with what a great catch she is, I know I'll have to clean up after her for the rest of my life. No thanks.

If you have children, taking care of them will also fall within the homemaking component. Some fathers will want to be hands-on in the early stages of infancy while others prefer to play with a clean baby who is not crying. Don't be disappointed if your man doesn't want to become deeply involved until the child starts walking and speaking.

To summarize, you need six qualities to maintain a healthy relationship so that a man will see you as a future wife. These qualities are also useful in maintaining a happy marriage as well since the dynamic is almost the same, at least until children enter the picture.

The first quality is to treat him as a leader. Your man does not want you to speak down to him or treat him as if you're his co-worker.

The second quality is to respect a man's alone time, and not confuse it with him being disinterested in you. It may seem weird to you, but men need to be completely alone and unmolested to regain the energy they expend when spending time with you or other people.

Third, you need to keep him sexually satisfied in a way that triggers his hunting instinct. Don't hesitate to be creative and kinky, especially after a year into the relationship when the initial spark begins to fade.

Fourth, you must maintain your appearance. It's much easier to leave a woman who is getting fat and unsightly than it is to leave one who is aging with elegance and grace. If anything, you should be improving your appearance as the relationship goes on.

Fifth, don't cheat or lie. Lying may get you through a sudden jam, but it will catch up with you and cause the relationship to end when you least expect it.

Lastly, take care of the home and children. If a man feels that you're lightening his load by maintaining a clean home and feeding his belly, he's far likelier to want to be your husband.

If you can excel in all of the above areas, it's almost guaranteed that a man who is in his settle-down stage will decide to marry you despite the punitive nature of divorce law. I know it's idealistic to expect you to excel at all six qualities, but the more of them you have, the better.

A problem may arise if one of the qualities conflicts with your personality or nature. Maybe you're too co-dependent and can't give a man his alone time. Maybe you have a thyroid problem that causes weight gain. Maybe you hate cleaning and would rather hire a maid. If you don't have one of the qualities, try to overcompensate with another. We all have our flaws, but you shouldn't be so flawed that a man sees you as only a source of sex. Sex will keep a man happy for a while, but it won't be enough to get him to marry you.

My last long-term girlfriend solidly hit three of the six qualities. She understood the importance of my alone time, kept me sexually satisfied, and maintained her appearance (she actually improved her appearance over the course of the relationship). Unfortunately, she had trouble treating me as a leader. She took so much pride in being "intelligent" that she attempted to challenge me on most of the decisions I made, which I found exhausting and frustrating when more than 98% of my decisions were correct. She was also lazy about the home. She had to be pushed into cleaning and cooking. I don't mind taking care of my woman, but at times I felt that I was feeding and nurturing her instead of the other way around. Most severely, I had issues with her cavorting with other men behind my back. I have no proof that these interactions were sexual, but they eroded my trust in her.

If she had respected my leadership, been honest, termi-nated her relationships with the men who wanted to sleep with her, and taken more care of the home, I'm confident that we'd be married today. My hope is that you already have shades of these six qualities, and you can bring them to the forefront without too much strain or effort.

Failures And Break-Ups

Unless you find a man who belongs to a tightly knit community, such as church, there won't be any external forces to keep you and him together. If there's a crisis in the relationship, his family and friends will take his side, and your family and friends will take yours. No one will intervene to act as a mediator. The culture won't help either, because it bombards both of you with never-ending messages of promiscuity, fun, and novelty, thereby ensuring that a conflict won't be resolved.

I know that when I'm dating a woman, I'm also dating all the things that directly and indirectly influence her. Essentially, I'm dating the entire world. When you're in a relationship with a man, you're really in a relationship with his best friends, his favorite websites, his parents, his social networking feeds, his favorite music, and so on. If these influences are pushing him away from monogamy and towards hedonism, the relationship won't have a chance.

You cannot isolate your man from the world. If he doesn't consciously and deliberately block out negative influences, your relationship will fail. This is why I believe that religion is so valuable for those who want monogamy, because no other factor can exert such a positive influence when it comes to marriage.

If a woman doesn't have religion in her life, I will be concerned that she won't place a high value on having a monogamous relationship and a stable family. Even if she is otherwise a good person, my experience shows that merely believing that God exists won't be enough to block out hedonistic influences—she must also be making sacrifices for the sake of her religious beliefs, such as attending church often or limiting her individualistic behavior in some way. If not, she will be prone to making decisions that feed her devil. The same applies to men— after all, I fed my devil for more than fifteen years.

It is now clear to me that religion provides the glue that is necessary to keep a man and a woman together. Love and passion are not enough. Without a godly aura enveloping your relationship, the chance of failure is wretchedly high, probably because we were not made to find our life partner through the mechanism of dating, a custom that is barely 100 years old. We were given biological tools to make us bond with one person, perhaps at a young age, and ride out that relationship for the rest of our lives. The modern dating scene, however, tells us that we must shop around and bond with several dozen people until we find "the one," but this strategy weakens our bonding glue as time passes, and we end up bitter, jaded, and isolated.

Religion and family are so intertwined that developing a relationship with God is the best way to increase your chances of finding a husband. Otherwise, you're in the casino playing the slot machines, hoping to hit the jackpot before you lose all your money, and this is assuming you don't get addicted to the rush of the game, of meeting new men and having them fawn over you.

The advice I have given you, particularly on screening men to find out whether they are in their settle-down stage, will provide you with the best chance of succeeding without the aid of religion. It's my wish that you don't experience relationships that fail after you've invested your time, love, and energy into them, but you're probably in a similar situation as me in that you've failed a number of times and need a way to move forward. The best you can do is to step inside the bright lights of the mating casino, fully armed with the advice and knowledge I've shared with you, and hope for a bit of luck so that you walk away a winner.

There are two common ways a long-term relationship can fail. The first is if your man gets cold feet about marriage. He may decide that the costs of marrying you outweigh the benefits. This could be because you are lacking in the six qualities that make for a good wife or he is worried about the consequences of divorce.

Not every man is cut out for marriage. Some don't believe that being with one woman will make them happy or that marriage is an essential part of a man's life. You will experience a lot of pain if the man you love decides not to marry you, but it's important that you don't waste any more of your time with such a man by thinking that he will "see the light" if you spend a few more months (or years) together, or that you will somehow persuade him to take the plunge.

If a man doesn't make the big leap and propose marriage by the end of the second year of your relationship, I don't see the point in waiting much longer. He must appreciate your needs and the fact that you have a biological clock. I'm always amazed when I hear of relationships that have gone on for five years or more without the man proposing marriage, but I can't entirely blame the man in these cases—he is comfortable having sex with the same girl and sees no reason to escalate his commitment if his girlfriend didn't expect marriage within a reasonable timeframe.

Ideally, you will demonstrate such stupendous wifely value that a man who wants a wife will *rush* to take you off the dating market and put babies in you. If you're merely "good enough for now" and fun in bed, he will never be motivated to marry you. This is why you need the proposal within two years so you will still have enough time to find another man if he decides to say no.

The second way a long-term relationship can fail is if your man cheats on you. The severity of the cheating can be judged by looking at *when* it happened. If it's less than a year into the relationship, before the sex became boring, this is a strong sign that he isn't in his settle-down phase and still has a high need for sexual variety. This is a deal-breaker, and you should end the relationship.

If the cheating happens much later, perhaps after you've had children and the passion has declined substantially, it's likely that he desired physical novelty, especially if his cheating didn't coincide with a decrease in his commitment to the family. If everything else is perfect in the home, and he hasn't been treating the family badly, it's more likely the cheating had a purely physical motive, and not a reason for you automatically to end the relationship.

Cheating is wrong, but I believe you should give your man a second chance if he cheated many years into the relationship instead of at the beginning. If I were a woman who was completely satisfied by my husband's apology, groveling, and chocolate gifts, and he is otherwise doing his duty in the marriage, I'd be more likely to forgive and forget than if I were in a relationship that hasn't yet made it to the altar. Since a man usually cheats for physical reasons, putting an effort into staying attractive and being creative in bed will decrease the likelihood of him thinking that being with another woman would be beneficial.

A man should be less forgiving if a woman cheats because it often stems from emotional reasons after her heart already checked out of the relationship, whereas a man usually just wanted a cheap orgasm. Also consider the worst-case outcome of either partner cheating: a man who impregnates his mistress will have to pay her monthly child-support payments, a terrible outcome, but a cheating woman may have another man's baby and trick her husband into raising that man's child as his own.

You're not likely to contemplate suicide if your man impregnates another woman, but a man will think of killing himself if it turns out that the child he loved and helped to raise is not his. I'm not saying that it doesn't matter if a man cheats on you, but female infidelity carries a higher price than male infidelity. This is why I advise men not to be forgiving of a cheating woman, no matter at what stage of the relationship she cheats, because doing so is practically the same as agreeing to be a cuckold. Besides, if a woman is cheating, it is likely that she will end the relationship soon because her heart is no longer in it.

If a long-term relationship ends, whether by your hand or his, you'll have a hard time dealing with it. Since a part of you grew with that man, a break-up will be like ripping off a piece of your skin, leaving a wound that refuses to heal. I wish I could give advice that will decrease the pain of a break-up, but there's nothing you can do to speed up the healing process besides grieving openly and giving yourself the time you need to restore your emotional health. Drowning your sorrows in alcohol or other men is not effective and will make the situation worse. Instead, it's best to understand what went wrong, admit any mistakes you made, and let the sadness work its way through you until the sunshine appears once again.

The problem with not accepting any responsibility for a break-up that was at least partially your fault is that you'll inevitably adopt an "all men are pigs" attitude and become bitter. The men you meet in the future will sense this negative attitude, making it less likely that they will put you in the potential wife box. If your ex was largely to blame for the relationship failing, criticize his behavior instead of all men: "He took me for granted and behaved in a way that hurt the relationship, but that doesn't mean that all men would have made the choices he did." The best coping mechanism is one that doesn't make it more difficult for you to connect with a good man in the future.

A man who just lost a girlfriend will be advised by his friends to sleep with a lot of women, but this doesn't work if those women are inferior versions of his ex, which is likely to be the case. The man will be reminded of her even more, keeping his wound raw. It's even worse if you sleep around because it lowers your wifely value for the right man who is bound to come along in the future.

Hopefully, you won't experience any serious relationship failures from this point on, but if you do, avoid the irrational conclusion that you'll never meet anyone again and are destined to be forever alone. Instead, take about six months off before starting again. Follow the advice in this book by maximizing the bait you put out to single men while fielding offers from the ones who are attracted to you. Always look on the bright side: you're a woman who will be hunted even if you put in only a little work to make it happen, unlike a man in the same position. Make yourself an attractive catch and wait patiently until the universe sends you the right match.

Conclusion

The hardest part of creating a family is meeting the right man, which is why much of this book is dedicated to overcoming that challenge. Once you've identified a man with the right values, and he is ready to settle down, there won't be many obstacles in the way of getting married besides the normal problems common to any intimate relationship.

The success of your mission to get married depends largely on the work you do *before* you meet a man, where you optimize your value and embrace the feminine to allow a masculine man to see you as his ideal wife. This involves discarding many of the bad habits and beliefs that you've accumulated from living in a world that has become bleak and sterile. It's not your fault that our broken culture has made it difficult for you to bond with a man, but you'll have to deal with the reality of the era you're living in if you want to avoid missing the boat to becoming a wife and mother. Following the advice in this book will at least enable you to attract and find a man who also wants to avoid the most damaging aspects of the culture.

Currently, I don't have much advice on how to raise children and grow old with your family. Perhaps if I have my own family one day, I'll be able to write a sequel to this book that focuses on parenting, but I hope I've provided you with enough guidance on how to meet a man, start a relationship with him, get a marriage proposal, and continue the relationship through an engagement and into the early years of marriage until your first pregnancy. If your relationship lasts until you become a mother, simply keep doing what you're doing. Trust your instincts, as long as they come from your angel.

My parting advice is to remember that the point of all this is not merely to get married, but to transcend the material world for the immaterial experiences of love, family, and a life that is compatible with your feminine essence. Yes, there is a ticking biological clock that pushes you to rush the process, but if you focus solely on beating your clock, you may lose sight of the importance of bonding with a man who is willing to sacrifice everything for you. Enjoy the journey of loving that man more than the destination of a wedding date, and understand that love and family are not so much an open-and-shut goal as they are an eternal fountain that will flow from your heart as long as you let it. Getting an engagement ring, a marriage contract, and a big home are merely the material side effects.

It is ironic that my advice has helped many men—and soon many women—to get married and have children, whereas that outcome has so far eluded me. Such is life, but even if I don't have children, I'm proud that I have been able to help others create their own families.

This book may not change the world, but I hope that it will help women who are ready to open their hearts and experience the very human journey of finding love and creating life. May God bless you on that journey.

Other books written by Roosh…

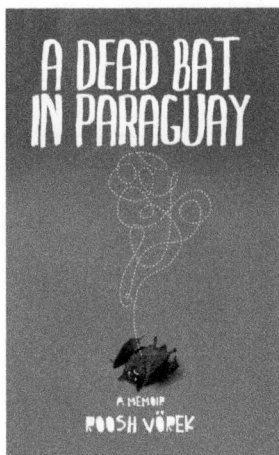

A Dead Bat In Paraguay: One Man's Peculiar Journey
Through South America

*'The honesty of the book shines through very brightly. The
book is fearless.'*

A Dead Bat In Paraguay is a true adventure story about
a 28-year-old man who decided that the best way he could
deal with his existential crisis was to sell his possessions,
quit his professional career as a scientist, and hop on a one-
way flight to Quito, Ecuador in order to visit every country
in South America.

He sincerely believed the trip would put him on a track
towards a more fulfilling life of excitement, intrigue, and
exotic women, away from his soulless corporate job in a
Washington D.C. suburb.

Instead, he humorously falls from one country to the
next, striking out repeatedly with the local women, getting

robbed, having dreams that became reality, self-diagnosing himself with a host of diseases, and suffering repeated bouts of stomach illness that made marathon bus rides superhuman feats of bodily strength.

Along the journey he chronicles the friendships, the women, and the struggles, including one fateful night in Paraguay that he thought would lead to his end.

'This is a really fun entertaining book, with a self-deprecating sense of humor. Imagine a young Larry David before he was famous, broke and traveling through South America.'

'It's one of the most honest and straightforward examples of what it's really like to travel by one's lonesome while a young single guy.'

'A extremely enjoyable book. Roosh writes in a deadpan straightforward way which is easy to get into.'

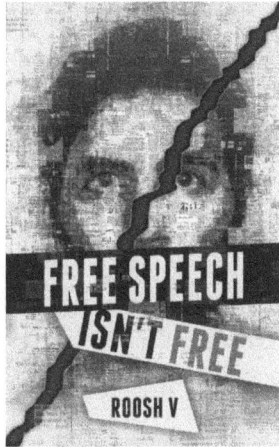

Free Speech Isn't Free: How 90 Men Stood Up
Against The Globalist Establishment -- And Won

*'His brutally honest and courageous writing does not fail
to hold the reader's attention and keep the pages turning.'*

Free speech may be your right, but unless you fight for
it, you'll lose it. That is the message of Free Speech Isn't
Free, which chronicles how organizing a lecture tour for
masculine men inserted Roosh into an unexpected free
speech fight spanning several continents, putting both him
and his family in danger from the globalist establishment
and their mob of deranged social justice warriors.

After becoming activated by mass-scale media distor-
tions and mayoral denouncements, the SJW mob in Canada
rose up against Roosh and his followers to halt his tour.
Roosh refused to cancel and set out to hold the lectures in
secret.

He shares how he fought back against the mob while
trying to come to terms with the globalist agenda that

they're controlled by. The well-informed men he met throughout the tour were critical in sharing hidden knowledge that put the agenda's puzzle pieces into place.

Even after the lecture, when Roosh tried to conduct happy hour meetings for his followers, a bigger worldwide outrage befell him, leading to the doxing of his family and threats to burn their house to the ground. Free Speech Isn't Free shares that story for the first time in a special epilogue, and what was going through the mind of a man who was the number one target for a 1984-inspired "two minutes of hate" that took place worldwide.

'When Roosh recounts his experience in Montreal, Toronto, and the Meetup Outrage, strap in your seat belts. You're in for quite a ride.'

How far will you go if the establishment attacks you for what you believe in? Are you ready to defend yourself if they come after your reputation, your job, and your family?

Free Speech Isn't Free shows what one man did when powerful groups tried to silence him, along with everything he learned during the most momentous months of his life that will help others be able to identify and defend against attacks within their own lives.

Bonuses included are the transcript of the "dangerous" speech that started it all, The State Of Man, and an important new article explaining how to keep yourself safe from social justice attacks.

'This is classic red pill reading.'

'A chronicle of a modern brave success and victory for free speech.'

Game: How To Meet, Attract, And Date Attractive
Women

Game teaches men a 9-step program for meeting and
attracting women in an age when smartphones, feminism,
and anti-masculinity propaganda have made connecting
with the opposite sex harder than ever.

*"I'm about half way done and wow, great work Roosh. I've
consumed a bunch of pick up material and I have to say,
this is some of the best stuff out there. Less routines, less
gimmicks, more real-life experience. Highly recommend."*

It is seminal work of a hyper-sexualized man who dedicated tens of thousands of hours into understanding women
and attracting them while fending off defamatory attacks
from mainstream feminists and fake news journalists who
want to criminalize healthy masculinity. Whether your goal
is to have fun in a big city with lots of women or fall in
love with only one before getting married, Game will help
you accomplish your goals in a way that keeps you safe

from degrading cultural winds that continue to divide men and women.

"I just finished the book, and all I can say, Roosh, is that it is criminally underpriced. It would be worth the cost at three times the price point, to start. By far your best work to date."

For more of my writing, visit my blog:

http://www.rooshv.com

Lightning Source UK Ltd.
Milton Keynes UK
UKHW010934231119
354069UK00002B/707/P